THE FIVE POINTS OF CALVINISM

WEIGHED AND FOUND WANTING

By George Bryson

THE WORD
FOR TODAY

x

x

P.O. Box 8000 • Costa Mesa CA 92628

The Five Points of Calvinism
Weighed and Found Wanting
by George Bryson

Published by **The Word for Today**
P.O. Box 8000, Costa Mesa, CA 92628
ISBN 0-936728-67-1

© 1996, 2002 The Word for Today

Table of Contents

Introduction

For more than a decade I was the host of a Christian talk show called 'Scripturally Speaking.' On many different occasions the topic of Calvinism in general, and the Five Points of Calvinism in particular, was introduced either by me, an in-studio guest, or a caller. I can clearly remember one discussion in which a Calvinist guest was debating with an Arminian caller over the question of whether or not predestination was taught in Scripture. When the question before us was simply a matter of affirming or denying predestination, I appeared to be on the side of my Calvinist guest.

The caller expressed surprise at my agreement with my guest because he incorrectly thought that I must have been a Calvinist because of this agreement. When I explained to him that I was not a Calvinist, the caller's surprise then turned to confusion.

Affirmation vs. Definition

My guest then admitted that he was also surprised, if not confused, for he too wrongly assumed I was a Calvinist because I agreed that predestination was taught in Scripture. The mistake both my Calvinist guest and Arminian caller had made was to assume that the distinctive of Calvinism is the Calvinist's affirmation of predestination. However, it is not the Calvinist's *affirmation* of predestination that distinguishes them from other Evangelicals. Rather it is the Calvinist's *definition* of predestination that distinguishes them from other Orthodox and Evangelical believers. The very popular Calvinist scholar, R. C. Sproul, in his book dedicated to defining and defending the Calvinist view of predestination, makes this same point. He says:

"Virtually all Christian churches have some formal doctrine of predestination.... If the Bible is the Word of God, not mere human speculation, and if God Himself declares that there is such a thing as predestination, then it follows that we must embrace some doctrine of predestination."[1]

The distinctives and doctrines of Calvinism are (relative to the doctrine of salvation) most evident in the Five Points of Calvinism. To understand the Five Points as Calvinists do, you must see them as the expression of the Calvinistic *definition* of predestination. The Calvinistic definition of predestination must in turn be viewed as the basis of the Calvinistic *doctrine* of salvation.

The Five Point Acrostic

A simple and common way to remember the Five Points of Calvinism is by using the acronym **TULIP.**

---

[1]   R.C. Sproul, *Chosen by God* (Wheaton, IL: Tyndale House Publishers Inc., 1986), 10.

T = Total Depravity

U = Unconditional Election

L = Limited Atonement

I = Irresistible Grace

P = Perseverance of the Saints

While acknowledging some value in using this acronym, Sproul also expresses some serious reservations. He says:

"This acrostic has helped many people remember the distinctives of Reformed Theology. Unfortunately, it has also caused a great deal of confusion and misunderstanding."[2]

5 Affirmations
or
5 Doctrines

When speaking about the Five Points, a Calvinist could either be referring to the brief affirmations associated with the acronym TULIP (i.e., Total Depravity, Unconditional Election, etc.) or the actual doctrines which are identified by these affirmations and for which the acronym is to be a reminder. You cannot understand the doctrine(s) of the Five Points by simply reading the much briefer affirmations associated with these doctrines. That is, there is a specific Calvinistic meaning that must be attached to these affirmations in order for them to be understood *Calvinistically*.

---

[2]   Ibid., 103.

This should not be taken as a criticism of the five affirmations for they were never intended to be an explanation. Thus each Calvinistic affirmation should be seen in relationship to a corresponding Calvinistic doctrine the way a chapter title is seen in relationship to the complete meaning and message of the chapter itself. Therefore, a simple statement of these Calvinistic affirmations, without an accurate Calvinistic explanation, can be very misleading.

Turning to Calvinists

Since it's the Five Points of *Calvinism* that we are going to discuss, it stands to reason that we turn to Calvinists for an interpretation and explanation of these five points.

Therefore, in the discussion which is to follow, I will rely (for an interpretation and explanation) heavily upon well-known Calvinist theologians, scholars, historical Calvinist documents, and of course, John Calvin himself. When discussing such concepts as Total Depravity, as used in the Five Points, we must remember that they are being used in a particular historical and Calvinistic context. A failure to keep this in mind will only lead to misunderstanding and confusion. In fact, this is the reason I believe many non-Calvinists can honestly (albeit, not accurately) call themselves one, two or three point Calvinists.

Soft vs. Hard

As we will momentarily see, there are what I call **softer** and **harder** forms of Calvinism. However, much of what passes for "moderate Calvinism" is not Calvinism at all. That is, many non-Calvinists see no problem with what they believe to be one or more of the Five Points (i.e., an affirmation such as Perseverance of the Saints) but they are interpreting these affirmations un-Calvinistically (or inconsistently with "authorial intent") and the actual doctrines of Calvinism to which these affirmations correspond.

Heart and Soul

It should also be noted that even though there is more to Calvinism than the Five Points, there is no Calvinism without the Five Points. Quite clearly they represent the heart and soul of Calvinism. Thus, to truly understand the Five Points is to understand Calvinism. To misunderstand the Five Points is to misunderstand Calvinism. According to the well-known Calvinist scholar Lorraine Boettner:

> *The Calvinistic system especially emphasizes five distinct doctrines. These are technically known as 'The Five Points of Calvinism' and they are the main pillars upon which the superstructure rests.*[3]

It therefore should go without saying that the superstructure of Calvinism, as a whole, is no more sure than the five pillars (i.e., Five Points) upon which it rests.

All or None

Boettner goes on to explain that:

> *These are not isolated and independent doctrines but are so inter-related that they form a simple, harmonious, self-consistent system; and the way they fit together as*

---

[3]   Lorraine Boettner, *The Reformed Doctrine of Predestination* (Phillipsburg, NJ: Presbyterian and Reformed Publishing Co., 1932), 59.

*component parts of a well-ordered whole
has won the admiration of thinking men of all
creeds. Prove any one of them true and all
the others will follow as logical and necessary
parts of the system. Prove any one of them
false and the whole system must be
abandoned. They are found to dovetail
perfectly one into the other.[4]*

Therefore it must also be stressed that any
attempt to single out one of the Five Points and to
try to interpret that point (or embrace it) as if it
stood alone, is also to interpret it *un*-Calvinistically.
As Calvinist theologian, Gise J. Van Baren says:

*The Five Points of Calvinism are closely
related. One point presupposes the others.[5]*

This does not mean that you cannot honestly or
even accurately (in a non-Calvinistic sense) say you
believe in "Total Depravity" or "Perseverance of the
Saints" and not in (let us say, as many do) "Limited
Atonement" or "Irresistible Grace." Rather, it means
that when you say you believe in one or more of the
Five Points without believing in them all, you
probably do not have the same thing in mind as
does the Calvinist. Thus you may not be talking
about the Five Points of Calvinism *per se*. Widely
respected advocate of the Five Points, J.I. Packer
cautions that:

*...The very act of setting out Calvinistic
soteriology (the doctrine of salvation) in the
form of five distinct points (a number due*

---

4   Ibid.

5   Gise J. Van Baren, *The Five Points of Calvinism* (Grand
        Rapids, MI: Reformed Free Publishing Assoc., 1976),
        91.

> merely to the fact that there were five
> Arminian points for the Synod of Dort to
> answer) tends to obscure the organic
> character of Calvinistic thought on this
> subject. For the five points, though separately
> stated, are really inseparable. They hang
> together; you cannot reject one without
> rejecting them all, at least in the sense in
> which the Synod meant them. For to
> Calvinism there is really only one point to be
> made in the field of soteriology.[6]

What Is the Point?

Packer reduces that one point to the words *"God saves sinners."* If that were really what the Five Points boiled down to, I would have no problem with the Five Points. However, despite what Packer says, as will be demonstrated, that "one point" of Calvinism can be likened to one coin which has two sides. Though seldom, if ever stated in such blunt terms, that "one point" can be summarized as follows:

> A person will either be saved or damned **for**
> all eternity because they were saved or
> damned **from** all eternity.

That is, according to Calvinism, God is just as responsible (and responsible in the same way) for damning the sinners He damns as He is for saving the sinners He saves. This will become especially clear in our discussion of the 2nd point of Calvinism (i.e., Unconditional Election).

---

[6]   J.I. Packer, quoted in *The Five Points of Calvinism*, David N. Steele and Curtis C. Thomas, (Phillipsburg, NJ: Presbyterian and Reformed Publishing Co., 1963), 22-23.

Why I Am Not a Calvinist

On many different occasions I have heard Calvinists say something like the following:

> *If only every true Christian with a working knowledge of Scripture understood Calvinism in general and the five points in particular, they would be five point Calvinists.*

However, as I hope it will become apparent, it is precisely because I understand Calvinism in general and the Five Points in particular that I am not a Calvinist—*of any kind*. I have spent more than 27 years in the serious study of Scripture. I could not even begin to calculate the hundreds of hours I have given to the study of Biblical, Systematic and Historical Theology. With great interest I have also carefully read the writings of Calvinists; both the so-called hyper-Calvinists as well as those considered more moderate. Just as Calvinists can and do understand non-Calvinistic systems of theology without embracing them, so non-Calvinists, such as myself, can understand Calvinism and still reject it as unbiblical.

If you understand Calvinism and still reject it, (as I do) some Calvinists will conclude that you must not really believe the Bible to be God's Word. Nothing could be further from the truth for myself and hundreds of thousands of others. Nevertheless, a rejection of Calvinism is interpreted by some Calvinists as a rejection of God's Word. Thus Boettner reasons that:

> *The Bible unfolds a scheme of redemption which is Calvinistic from beginning to end, and these doctrines are taught with such inescapable clearness that the question is*

> *settled for all those who accept the Bible as
> the Word of God.*[7]

Other Calvinists (perhaps most) see the *rejection*
of Calvinism by Evangelical Christians as the result
of the *acceptance* of Arminianism.

Non-Arminian Reasons

However, for the record, I wish to make it clear
that I am not in disagreement with Calvinism for
"Arminian" reasons. I say this because a common
myth perpetuated by some Calvinists as well by
some Arminians is that if you are an Evangelical
Christian and not a Calvinist, you must be an
Arminian, at the very least by default. While I agree
with Calvinists and Arminians that these two
systems of theology are mutually exclusive and
therefore cannot both be true, I emphatically
disagree that these are the only Evangelical or
Orthodox options. However, I am not writing to
explain why I am not an Arminian (or a theological
hybrid called Calminian). Someday I would like to
write such a book. However, this is not my present
concern.

Moderate Calvinists?

I should also point out that many people who
call themselves moderate Calvinists will not identify
with the Calvinists I rely upon to represent what I
believe to be *authentic* Calvinism. In some cases it
will be due to the fact that many people mistakenly
call themselves Calvinists because they have bought
into this notion that if you are not an Arminian you

---

[7]   Lorraine Boettner, *The Reformed Doctrine of
Predestination*, 52.

must be a Calvinist. Others simply interpret the Five Points in a non-Calvinistic way. Often it is a combination of both.

Primary Purpose

My primary purpose for writing this book is to encourage the reader who might be inclined to seriously consider embracing Calvinism to first subject the Five Points to what I believe is (for Calvinism) the "harsh" light of Scripture. As I see it, a careful study of Scripture is not all that kind to the Five Points. If you are already a Calvinist, or think that you might be, I only ask that you be certain that you are judging the Five Points in the light of Scripture and not simply interpreting Scripture in keeping with the Five Points.

A Little History

For those interested in a little history of the Five Points, it should be understood that they are not only a reflection of the views of the reformer John Calvin, but also of Saint Augustine. Just as the Synod of Dort, (the synod which first formally presented these points as the Five Points of Calvinism), was a Calvinistic Synod, so John Calvin was an Augustinian. This is especially true with regard to the Augustinian view of predestination and its bearing upon the salvation of the elect and the damnation of the unelect. Co-author of one of several books called *The Five Points of Calvinism* and written to explain and defend Calvinism, Professor Herman Hanko says that:

> *In fact, our fathers at Dordrecht knew well that these truths set forth in the Canons could not only be traced back to the Calvin*

Reformation; they could be traced back to the theology of Saint Augustine who lived almost a millennium before Calvin did his work in Geneva. For it was Augustine who had originally defined these truths. Calvin himself, again and again, pays tribute to the work of Augustine and points out that what he is saying has been said before him by the Bishop of Hippo. The Synod of Dordrecht was conscious of this.[8]

Boettner agrees. He says:

It was Calvin who wrought out this system of theological thought with such logical clearness and emphasis that it has ever since borne his name. He did not, of course, originate the system but only set forth what appeared to him to shine forth so clearly from the pages of Holy Scripture. Augustine had the essentials of the system a thousand years before Calvin was born, and the whole body of the leaders of the Reformation movement taught the same. But it was given to Calvin with his deep knowledge of Scripture, his keen intellect and systematizing genius, to set forth and defend these truths more clearly and ably than had been done before.[9]

Calvinist theologian R. Laird Harris states that:

Although Calvin gave the Reformed doctrine its most thorough formulation, the theology had long been held. Calvin would have

---

8   H. Hanko and H.C. Hoeksema and J. Van Baren, *The Five Points of Calvinism* (Grand Rapids, MI: Reformed Free Publishing Association, 1976), 10.

9   Lorraine Boettner, *The Reformed Doctrine of Predestination*, 3-4.

*been the first to deny its novelty.... Indeed
Calvinism is often called Augustinianism.*[10]

Is It Scriptural?

Of course this, in and of itself, does not say
anything good or bad about the Five Points. As
Calvinist writers, Steele and Thomas state:

> *The question of supreme importance is not
> how the system under consideration came to
> be formulated into five points, or why it was
> named Calvinism, but rather is it supported
> by Scripture? The final court of appeal for
> determining the validity of any theological
> system is the inspired, authoritative Word of
> God. If Calvinism can be verified by clear
> and explicit declaration of Scripture, then it
> must be received by Christians; if not, it must
> be rejected.*[11]

Boettner concurs as follows:

> *The Scriptures are the final authority by which
> systems are judged. In all matters of
> controversy between Christians the Scriptures
> are accepted as the highest court of
> appeal.*[12]

The much respected Calvinist Theologian,
Charles Hodge, said that:

> *It is the duty of every theologian to
> subordinate his theories to the Bible, and
> teach not what seems to him to be true or*

---

[10]   R. Laird Harris, "Calvinism," *The Wycliffe Bible
        Encyclopedia*, vol. 1 (Chicago, IL: Moody Press, 1975),
        293.

[11]   David N. Steele and Curtis C. Thomas, *The Five
        Points of Calvinism*, 24.

[12]   Lorraine Boettner, *The Reformed Doctrine of
        Predestination*, 51.

> *reasonable, but simply what the Bible teaches.[13]*

To this I heartily agree. Therefore in the last half of this book we will carefully consider what Scripture has to say on the matters to which the Five Points speak.

What the Five Points Are *Not* Saying

One final word before moving on to explain what Calvinists have in mind when they speak of the Five Points of Calvinism. As noted earlier, many Evangelicals mistakenly think they accept one or more of three of the Five Points and thus truly believe themselves to be moderate (or one, two or three point) Calvinists. An example of what I mean is found in an article titled "Baptists may split over Calvinism." The author of this article rightly observes that:

> *The five cardinal doctrines of strict Calvinism are: Total Depravity of man, unconditional election, limited atonement, irresistible grace, and Perseverance of the Saints.[14]*

However he immediately goes on to say that:

> *Most Southern Baptists would have little quarrel with three of these points: Total Depravity (**all have sinned**), unconditional election (**the saved are chosen by God without regard for their own merit**), and*

---

[13]   Charles Hodge, quoted in Lorraine Boettner, *The Reformed Doctrine of Predestination*, 50.

[14]   Mark Wingfield, "Resurgent Calvinism Renews Debate Over Chance for Heaven," *Baptists Today*, Feb. 16, 1995 (Vol. 13, No 4).

*Perseverance of the Saints (**once saved always saved**).*[15]

As long as Christians think the Calvinist doctrine of Total Depravity is simply that all have sinned; or that the Calvinist distinctive of unconditional election is that salvation is unmerited; or even that the Calvinistic view of perseverance can be equated with the doctrine of "once saved always saved," they will continue to incorrectly think of themselves as Calvinists.

While Calvinists, along with non-Calvinists, believe all have sinned, salvation is without merit and once saved always saved, these are not exclusive to or even the distinctives of Calvinism or its Five Points.

Explanation Before Evaluation

Thus it should be obvious that without a clear and accurate explanation of the Five Points, a fair and scriptural evaluation is not possible. Therefore, in this next section of the book (the first of two major sections), I have attempted to allow (as much as possible) Five Point Calvinists to explain what they have in mind when they speak about such doctrines as Total Depravity and Unconditional election.

---

[15]   Ibid.

I
Total Depravity
Explained

Among Calvinists, there are basically two schools of thought (i.e., hard and soft) with regard to Total Depravity. However, the difference between authentic Calvinists (as it relates to depravity) is one of *degree* and not *kind.*

The Soft View

Some Calvinists contend that the unregenerate (one not born again) is sinful in every area of his life, but not necessarily as sinful as he can be. Steele and Thomas state that:

> When Calvinists speak of man as being totally depraved, they mean that man's nature is corrupt, perverse, and sinful throughout. The adjective "total" does not mean that each sinner is as totally or completely corrupt in his actions and thoughts as it is possible for him to be. Instead, the word "total" is used to indicate that the whole of man's being has been affected by sin. The corruption extends to every part of man, his body and soul; sin has

*affected all (the totality) of man's faculties
—his mind, his will, etc.*[16]

Boettner says essentially the same thing as follows:

*This doctrine of Total Inability...does not
mean that all men are equally bad, nor that
any man is as bad as he could be, nor that
anyone is entirely destitute of virtue.... His
corruption is extensive but not necessarily
intensive.*[17]

Sproul goes so far as to say that:

*Total Depravity is a very misleading term. The
concept of Total Depravity is often confused
with the idea of utter depravity.... Total
Depravity is not utter depravity. Utter
depravity would mean that we are as sinful
as we can possibly be. We know that is not
the case. No matter how much each of us
has sinned, we are able to think of worse sins
that we could have committed. Even Adolf
Hitler refrained from murdering his mother.*[18]

The Hard View

To this point, I, along with most other
mainstream Evangelicals, would agree. However,
other Calvinists see the soft view of Total Depravity
as a compromise. Hanko believes that "total" means
"absolute." He says the Synod of Dort intended us
to understand: "that man *is* just as sinful as he can
be." (italics mine)

---

[16]   David N. Steele and Curtis C. Thomas, *The Five
        Points of Calvinism*, 25.

[17]   Lorraine Boettner, *The Reformed Doctrine of
        Predestination*, 61.

[18]   R.C. Sproul, *Chosen by God*, 103-104.

Hanko goes on to say that:

When Calvin and the fathers of Dort insisted that depravity was total, they knew what words mean. And they knew that "total" means precisely that.[19]

Hoeksema says:

The distinction between absolute and Total Depravity has in late years been applied to men in their fallen and corrupt state. They make this distinction in order to make clear how a totally depraved sinner can still do good works. Man, according to this view, is totally depraved, but not absolutely depraved. And because he is not absolutely depraved, he is able to do good before God in his natural state. Of course, with this philosophy they fail to make clear what they really want to explain. For a totally depraved man is after all evil and corrupt in his whole nature, in all his thinking, willing, desiring, and acting; and the problem still remains, even with the distinction between total and absolute depravity, how such a totally depraved man can bring forth good fruits. Besides, if one would make the distinction between total and absolute depravity, the distinction must certainly be applied in a different way. For by Total Depravity is meant that man by nature in all his existence, with all his heart and mind and soul and strength, has become a servant of sin, and that he is

---

[19]   H. Hanko and H.C. Hoeksema and J. Van Baren, *The Five Points of Calvinism*, 18.

entirely incapable of doing good and inclined to all evil.[20]

The Calvinistic Heidelberg Catechism asks the question:

Are we then so corrupt that we are wholly incapable of doing any good, and inclined to all wickedness?

Apparently, in agreement with Hanko and Hoeksema, it answers:

Indeed we are; except we are regenerated (born again) by the Spirit of God.[21]

John Calvin also seemed to take the harder view when he said,

...Our nature is not only utterly devoid of goodness, but so prolific in all kinds of evil, that it can never be idle. Those who term it concupiscence use a word not very inappropriate, provided it were added, (this, however, many will by no means concede), that everything which is in man, from the intellect to the will, from the soul even to the flesh, is defiled and pervaded with this concupiscence; or, to express it more briefly, that the whole man is in himself **nothing else but concupiscence**.[22] *(emphasis mine)*

---

20   Herman Hoeksema, *Reformed Dogmatics* (Grand Rapids, MI: Reformed Free Publishing Association, [reprinted] 1985), 252.

21   Heidleberg Catechism, quoted in *The Five Points of Calvinism*, H. Hanko and H.C. Hoeksema and J. Van Baren, 23.

22   John Calvin, *Institutes of the Christian Religion*, book 2, chap. 1, sec. 8 (Grand Rapids, MI: Eerdmans Publishing Co., [reprinted] 1993), 218.

However, it is extremely important that we not reduce the Calvinistic view of Total Depravity to merely how sinful the unregenerate are. That, as I said before, is simply a question of degree. Some Arminians, and indeed John Wesley himself, believed unregenerate man to be every bit as depraved as did Calvin. Concerning the effects (and the degree) of the fall on human nature, Wesley asked:

Was there not good mingled with the evil? Was there not light intermixed with the darkness?

He then answered,

No, none at all.

To support his contention he then quoted the following Scriptures:

*God saw that the whole imagination of the heart of man was **only evil**.*

*And "In his flesh dwelt **no good thing** ." (emphasis mine)*

Wesley went on to say concerning the nature of man after the fall,

*that it was **only evil continuously**, every year, every day, every hour, every moment. He **never deviated into good**.[23]*

Thus it would appear that Wesley, the architect of contemporary Arminianism, actually sided with the harder view of Calvinism as to how depraved fallen man is. Therefore if we are to find the distinctive of Total Depravity in Calvinism we will

---

[23]   John Wesley, *The Works of John Wesley*, vol. 6, (Zondervan, Grand Rapids, MI, 58-59), 56-57.

have to look some place other than in the degree to which man has fallen and is a sinner.

Again, the real distinctive of Depravity in Calvinism is not in what we do because we are Totally Depraved (or in how much or how badly we do it), nor even in what we *cannot* do if we mean by this the inability of fallen man to do good.

The *Inoperable* Will of Man

What we cannot do because of Total Depravity, from a Calvinistic perspective, is of course very important to a Calvinistic definition of Depravity, especially as it is relates to a gospel presentation directed at the unregenerate. That is, Calvinistically speaking, the unregenerate are not only unable to do good (as well as unable to refrain from doing bad) spiritually in a general sense, but more specifically, they are *unable* to respond to God or the Gospel (to any degree) while in an unregenerate state or before being born again.

According to this view, the will of unregenerate man (in so far as responding to God, the Gospel, etc., is concerned) is dead and therefore *inoperable.* This idea of an inoperable will is very crucial to a complete understanding of a Calvinistic definition of Total Depravity.

Thus, according to Calvinism, the unregenerate man cannot receive Christ as Lord and Savior, and cannot believe in Christ or believe the Gospel preached to him, *as* an unregenerate man. He cannot do anything to accept the free gift of eternal life offered to him and thereby be saved. The outspoken Calvinist pastor and author James Boice asks:

> *What does it mean when it says that we are "dead in trespasses and sins"? Does it mean that we are really dead so far as any ability to respond to God or to choose is concerned?*[24]

Not only does Boice go to great lengths to "prove" that a lost person cannot respond to God and His offer of salvation (while lost), but he even seems to suggest that those who believe the lost can believe and receive (while lost) cannot see or find the way of salvation either. However, Boice goes on to say that,

> *If we will renounce all thoughts of such ability, He will show us the way of salvation through Christ and lead us to salvation.*[25]

If we are to take this statement seriously, it would mean that we would have to agree with the Calvinist on this point before we could even come to Christ. Nevertheless, while Calvinists believes the regenerate (i.e., those born again) are called to preach the gospel of salvation to the unregenerate, they also hold that the unregenerate cannot respond to the gospel while they are unregenerate.

Spiritual Birth Before Saving Faith

Again, and Calvinistically speaking, because of the effect of Depravity on the unregenerate, those who are to be regenerated must be regenerated (i.e.,

---

[24]   James Boice, *Foundations of the Christian Faith* [Revised Edition] (Downers Grove, IL: Inter-Varsity Press, 1986), 209.

[25]   Ibid., 316.

born again) so that they can believe in Christ. You must be born again first. Only after spiritual rebirth can you have and exercise saving faith from a Calvinist's point of view. No definition of depravity that allows faith before regeneration can legitimately claim to be in agreement with the 1st point. Ironically, and as we will see later, there is reason to believe that Calvin believed that faith comes before regeneration. Nevertheless, regeneration before faith has become *The Distinctive* of a Calvinistic definition of Total Depravity.

On the subject of the new birth, Calvinist Theologian Allan R. Killen states:

> *Reformed theologians...place **regeneration before faith**, pointing out that the Holy Spirit must bring new life before the sinner can by God's enabling exercise faith and accept Jesus Christ.*[26] *(emphasis mine)*

Sproul says that:

> *A **cardinal** point of Reformed theology is the maxim: "Regeneration precedes faith."*[27] *(emphasis mine)*

This is, of course, exactly opposite of what almost all non-Calvinist Evangelicals believe.

Total Depravity = Total Inability

So important to Calvinists is this notion that the unregenerate are *unable* to believe the Gospel or to receive Christ in their unregenerate state, that most Calvinists use the term Total Inability and Total

---

[26]   Allan R. Killan, "Regeneration," *The Wycliffe Bible Encyclopedia*, vol. 2, 1449.

[27]   R.C. Sproul, *Chosen by God*, 72.

Depravity interchangeably. Steele and Thomas explain that:

> *Because of the fall, man is unable of himself to savingly believe the gospel. The sinner is dead, blind, and deaf to the things of God; his heart is deceitful and desperately corrupt. His will is not free, it is in bondage to his evil nature, therefore, he will not -indeed he cannot- choose good over evil in the spiritual realm. Consequently, it takes much more than the Spirit's assistance to bring a sinner to Christ —it takes regeneration by which the Spirit makes the sinner alive and gives him a new nature. Faith is not something man contributes to salvation, but is itself a part of God's gift of salvation —it is God's gift to the sinner, not the sinner's gift to God.*[28]

In saying that "it takes much more than the Spirit's assistance to bring a sinner to Christ," Steele and Thomas are debunking what Arminians and other non-Calvinists refer to as prevenient grace. Simply stated, prevenient grace is the supernatural (or otherwise) assistance non-Calvinist evangelicals believe God extends to the unregenerate in order to free him enough (i.e., from the effects of depravity) so that he is able (if he is willing) to receive and believe in Jesus Christ.

The Westminster Confession states:

---

[28]   David N. Steele and Curtis C. Thomas, *The Five Points of Calvinism*, 16.

Man, by his fall into a state of sin, hath wholly lost all ability of will to any spiritual good accompanying salvation.[29]

Steele and Thomas add that:

As a result of Adam's transgression, men are born in sin and by nature are spiritually dead; therefore, if they are to become God's children and enter His kingdom, they must be born anew of the Spirit.[30]

From Death to Life
Without Faith in Christ

The point is that you go from death to life without placing faith in Christ. Faith in Christ, from a Calvinist perspective, comes with that life but is neither needed nor possible before that life begins.

It is perhaps best to refer to the inoperable will of the unregenerate—relative to receiving Christ, believing the Gospel when it is preached, or responding to God positively in any way—as the *implication* of Total Depravity in Calvinistic thinking and theology.

Allow me to distinguish between what I am referring to as the *implication* of Total Depravity, and the *significance* of Total Depravity. The implication of Total Depravity is the same for everyone, elect and unelect alike, according to Calvinism. That is, as long as an individual is in an unregenerate state, he cannot believe in Christ.

---

[29] *The Westminster Confession of Faith* [chapter 9, section 3].

[30] David N. Steele and Curtis C. Thomas, *The Five Points of Calvinism*, 25.

Yet, the significance of Total Depravity is drastically different for the elect as opposed to the unelect. This we will consider in the next chapter on Unconditional Election.

The Distinctive of Calvinistic Depravity

However, before we move on, allow me to reiterate the most important Calvinistic distinctive relative to Total Depravity. In Herman Hoeksema's *Reformed Dogmatics* he argues that, with regard to the logical order of the application of salvation, the first thing God does is regenerate the elect. Only after a man is born again can God effectually call him. Only after and as a result of this regeneration and effectual calling can he exercise saving faith in Jesus Christ. And because the calling is effectual, the faith that follows regeneration is inevitable.[31]

The importance of this order (i.e., regeneration *before* faith) from a Calvinistic perspective will become increasingly clear as we proceed in our discussion of the other points. However, Sproul probably speaks for all Calvinists on this matter when he says:

> In regeneration, God changes our hearts. He gives us a new disposition, a new inclination. He plants a desire for Christ in our hearts. We can never trust Christ for our salvation unless we first desire Him. This is why we said earlier that **regeneration precedes faith**...[32] (emphasis his)

---

[31]   Herman Hoeksema, *Reformed Dogmatics*, 451.

[32]   R.C. Sproul, *Chosen by God*, 118.

It should be kept in mind that the relationship and order of regeneration to faith is often, if not usually, discussed by Calvinists in the context of the Calvinist doctrine of Total Depravity. In fact, the chapter of Sproul's book explaining what is meant by Total Depravity and what he prefers to call "radical corruption" is titled "REBIRTH AND FAITH."

At the risk of getting side-tracked, I should also point out that some Calvinists distinguish between:

"...Regeneration in the deepest and narrowest sense of the word," and "...Regeneration in the broader sense of the word."[33]

I am not sure if it is the narrowest or the broader sense of regeneration that Hoeksema had in mind when he said that:

> *...Independent of age... regeneration... can take place in the smallest of infants. We may even take for granted that in the sphere of the covenant of God He usually regenerates His elect children from infancy.*[34]

If regeneration can occur during infancy what about salvation? Calvin reasons that:

> *...Infants that are to be saved (and that some are saved at this stage is certain) must, without question, be previously regenerated by the Lord.*[35]

---

[33]   H. C. Hoeksema, *Reformed Dogmatics*, 462-464.

[34]   Ibid., 462-464.

[35]   Calvin, *Institutes of the Christian Religion*, 542.

It must be deduced then that somehow these same infants must also place their faith in Christ, while infants, since on the one hand regeneration must precede (and is required to produce) faith, and on the other hand, Faith in Christ is essential to being saved by Christ. That is, if the elect infants are saved by Grace through faith, then they must exercise that faith after regeneration and before salvation according to Calvinism or before regeneration, according to Calvin. In either case, it is faith in Christ in the womb. This gives new meaning to the expression "Child-like Faith." If you ask "How can this be?" Calvin would answer:

> *This is as possible for (God) as it is as wondrous and **incomprehensible** to us.*[36]

Incidentally, if you are among the elect you may be wondering about your children. How can you know if they will or will not be saved? If only the elect can be regenerated and only the regenerated can be saved, is there anyway of knowing if our own children will be elect? According to Calvin (but I am not sure about Calvinism itself), it would appear that God does have (at least in one sense) spiritual grand-children after all. That is, according to Calvin:

> *Our children, before they are born, God declares He adopts for His own when He promises He will be a God to us, and to our seed after us. In this promise their salvation is included.*[37]

---

[36]   Ibid.

[37]   Ibid., 526.

If this is true, we need not concern ourselves with our children or our children's children, etc., etc., etc. Why? Because if we are elect, our children are also elect, which also means their children are elect, and so on until our lineage comes to an end. While a Calvinist may find comfort in this view, he needs to flip this coin over to see what is on the other side. If it follows that your children are elect and will be saved if you are one of the elect, would it not also follow, that if your child never believes in Jesus Christ, he proves he was not elect. If he proves not to be elect, he proves you are not elect. If you prove not to be elect, your father could not have been elect either. This election domino must logically fall in both directions.

Predestination Permeates

Finally, before proceeding to a discussion of the 2nd point, it will probably be helpful to briefly make mention of the Calvinist definition and corresponding doctrine of predestination as it relates to the Calvinist view of Total Depravity. As stated in the introduction, the Calvinist view of predestination permeates all five points.

With some of the points, especially the 2nd (unconditional election) and the 4th (irresistible grace), the part a Calvinistic definition of predestination plays is more obvious. However, according to leading Calvinists it is clearly central to all five points. Thus Total Depravity must also be seen through a special "predestinarian" lens. John H. Gerstner, the man Sproul calls "...king of the Calvinists," and who he says "is to predestination what Einstein is to physics or what Arnold Palmer is to Golf."[38] said that we can:

> *Trace four steps to predestination. First, there is the Total Depravity of mankind. The 2nd step is the resultant inability. This necessitates the 3rd step, the divine initiative in the soul. And that brings us to the 4th and last step, predestination itself.[39]*

It is evident that what Gerstner refers to as the first two steps leading to predestination (i.e., Total Depravity and the resultant total inability) are what we have discussed as the 1st point. His 3rd step (what he calls the divine initiative in the soul) *is* or *leads to* regeneration. And as we have been repeatedly reminded, this regeneration must, because of depravity, come before a person can exercise saving faith in Jesus Christ. Another and perhaps more succinct way of stating what Gerstner is saying is as follows;

> *The 1st point (Total Depravity), and all that is implied or necessitated because of Total Depravity, leads unavoidably to the Calvinist doctrine of predestination.*

I hasten to add however that it is the Calvinistic definition and doctrine of predestination that initially leads most Calvinists to believe as they do about Total Depravity as well as the other four points.

As Sproul says:

---

[38]   R.C. Sproul, *Chosen by God*, 12.

[39]   John H. Gerstner, *A Predestination Primer* (Winona Lake, IN: Alpha Publications, [reprinted 1979]), 13.

*The Reformed view of **predestination** teaches that before a person can choose Christ his heart must be changed. He must be born again...one does not first believe, then become reborn...[40] (Emphasis mine)*

---

[40]   R.C. Sproul, *Chosen by God*, 72.

II
Unconditional Election
Explained

If Total Depravity says that the unregenerate *cannot* believe the Gospel or receive Christ, or in any way respond positively to God in his unregenerate state, Unconditional Election says that this does not matter (for the unregenerate elect). For God has, from all eternity, elected some to be saved unconditionally. Calvinistically speaking, faith is therefore not a *condition* for the salvation of the lost but a **consequence** of regeneration for the elect. In other words, faith in Christ is not a **requirement** for being born again but a **result** of being born again, according to Calvinism.

Steele and Thomas explain:

God's choice of certain individuals unto salvation before the foundation of the world rested solely in His own sovereign will. His choice of particular sinners was not based on any foreseen response or obedience on their part, such as faith, repentance, etc. On the contrary, God gives faith and repentance to each individual whom He selected... These acts are the result, not the cause of God's choice. Thus, God's choice of the sinner, and not the sinner's choice of Christ, is the ultimate cause of salvation.[41]

Hanko explains:

Election is, therefore, that decree of God which He makes, by which, with sovereign freedom, He chooses to Himself a people, upon whom He determines to set His love, whom He rescues from sin and death through Jesus Christ, unto Himself in everlasting glory. This election is sovereign —God's sovereign and free choice. This election is eternal even as God's counsel is eternal. This election is unchangeable even as God's counsel is unchangeable. This election is efficacious so that the decree of election itself is, through Christ, the power by which the elect are actually saved.[42]

Steele and Thomas agree that:

The doctrine of election declares that God, before the foundation of the world, chose certain individuals from among the fallen members of Adam's race to be the objects of His undeserved favor. These, and these only, He purposed to save. God could have chosen to save all men (for He had the power and authority to do so) or He could have chosen to save none (for He was under no obligation to show mercy to any) - but He did neither. Instead He chose to save some and to exclude others. His eternal choice of particular sinners unto salvation was not based upon any foreseen act or response on

---

[41]   David N. Steele and Curtis C. Thomas, *The Five Points of Calvinism*, 16-17.

[42]   H. Hanko and H.C. Hoeksema and J. Van Baren, *The Five Points of Calvinism*, 33.

*the part of those selected, but was based
solely on His own good pleasure and
sovereign will. Thus election was not
determined by, or conditioned upon,
anything that men would do, but resulted
entirely from God's self-determined
purpose.*[43]

What About the Unelect?

If the implication of Depravity for the
unregenerate elect (i.e., a dead and inoperable will)
is answered by Unconditional Election (i.e., it does
not matter), then Unconditional Election for the
unelect says, "Tough luck."

Nevertheless, as with Total Depravity, there are
two schools of thought among Calvinists with
regard to Unconditional Election—as it relates to
reprobation, or not being elected.

The Softer View

The softer view says that while God elects to
save some, He does not elect to damn the rest. The
great English Calvinist preacher, Charles Spurgeon
said:

*Your damnation is your own election, not
God's.*

*We are lost willfully and willingly, lost
perversely and utterly, but still lost of our own
accord, which is the worst kind of being lost.*

*From the Word of God I gather that
damnation is all of man, from top to
bottom,....He that perishes chooses to
perish...*

---

[43]   David N. Steele and Curtis C. Thomas, *The Five
Points of Calvinism*, 30.

> *We hold tenaciously that salvation is all of grace, but we also believe with equal firmness that the ruin of man is entirely the result of his own sin. It is the will of God that saves; it is the will of man that damns.*
>
> *All true theology is summed in these two short sentences: Salvation is all of the grace of God. Damnation is all of the will of man.*[44]

Sproul refers to this softer view of election and non-election "as Orthodox Calvinism's view" and calls it "positive-negative predestination." He explains that:

> *The Reformed view teaches that God positively or actively intervenes in the lives of the elect to insure their salvation. The rest of mankind He leaves to themselves.*[45]

The Harder View

Sproul refers to the harder view as "Hyper-Calvinism's view of double predestination" and characterizes it as "positive-positive predestination."[46]

By this he means the harder position says that God actively intervenes or elects some for Hell just as He elects some for Heaven.

It would seem that Steele and Thomas come down on the side of the soft view of election, or single predestination, while Hanko, Hoeksema, and Van Baren agree with the Harder view, or double

---

[44]   Charles Spurgeon [compiled by Tom Carter], *Spurgeon at His Best* (Grand Rapids, MI: Baker Book House, 1988), 48, 62, 122.

[45]   R.C. Sproul, *Chosen by God*, 142-143.

[46]   Ibid., 143.

predestination. If we allow John Calvin to settle the matter, it appears that the harder view is the more authentic Calvinistic view—despite Sproul's characterization of his view as "Orthodox," and the harder view as "Hyper." Calvin said:

> *Many professing a desire to defend the Deity from an invidious charge admit the doctrine of election, but deny that any one is reprobated...This they do ignorantly and childishly, since there could be no election without its opposite reprobation. God is said to set apart those whom he adopts for salvation. It were most absurd to say, that he admits others fortuitously, or that they by their industry acquire what election alone confers on a few. Those therefore whom God passes by he reprobates, and that for no other cause than he is pleased to exclude them from the inheritance which he predestines to his children.*[47]

The Cause of Exclusion

When Calvin says that reprobation results from "no other cause than" God's pleasure "to exclude them," he admitted more than what most Calvinists like to think or talk about. That is, Calvinistically speaking, the lost will not be eternally lost for committing sins or being Depraved, any more than the saved will be eternally saved for believing the Gospel or receiving Christ. That is, Calvinism asserts that the elect are eventually, ultimately and inevitably saved unconditionally, just as the unelect are eventually, ultimately and inevitably lost unconditionally.

---

[47]   John Calvin, *Institutes of the Christian Religion*, book 3, chap 23, sec 1, 225.

Even though most Calvinists **will say** that the unelect are damned because they deserved to be, the logical implication of Calvinism says otherwise. Since the unelect were not elected to be saved, they were never meant to be regenerated, to believe, to be saved, or to be anything other than Totally Depraved and lost forever. Calvinistically speaking, unregenerate man can no more *be blamed* for his damnation than regenerate man can *take credit* for his salvation. According to Calvinism, as salvation is a consequence of election so damnation is a consequence of reprobation. And since the unregenerate are reprobate as a result of a choice made by God alone, how could they be responsible for their lostness and ultimate and inevitable damnation?

Faith—Not a Factor

What this means is that God and not man decided who would be reprobated just as He decided who would be elected. And, according to Calvinism, He did this without regard to the question of faith in Christ or the sinfulness of man.

Thus, Calvinistic Election says to the unregenerate elect, "Don't Worry, your Depravity is no obstacle to salvation," and to the unelect, "Too bad, you have not been predestined for salvation but damnation."

Many Calvinists will no doubt claim that this is a misrepresentation of their position. As one Calvinist said to me, "Read my lips, I believe that the unelect deserve to be damned forever, and are damned forever because they deserve to be." However, such a statement reveals that he does not seem to grasp the implication of his own position. Perhaps an illustration will help.

Why the Unelect Are Not Elect

Suppose you are offered some chocolates from a box of chocolates. While gazing into the box, you decide that there is nothing in any of the chocolates to make you want to pick one chocolate over another. Nevertheless, you choose some of the chocolates, and some of the chocolates you do not choose. You may have a reason for picking some and not others, but the reason has nothing to do with the individual chocolates themselves. It stands to reason then, if there is nothing in the chocolates that affected your decision to pick one piece of chocolate over the others, then there is also nothing in the ones you do not pick to affect your decision to *not* pick them.

In like manner if there is nothing in or about the elect to distinguish them for selection—no criterion related to them—then there can be nothing in or about the unelect that affects God's decision to not elect them.

Good Fortune vs. Misfortune

As stated earlier, Calvinistically speaking, if it is your good fortune to be among the elect you will be saved *for* all eternity because you were in effect (and unconditionally) saved *from* all eternity. Even so, if it is your misfortune to be among the unelect you will be damned *for* all eternity because in effect (and unconditionally) you were damned *from* all eternity.

For those tempted to think that I am misrepresenting Calvinism a few words from John

Calvin should demonstrate that such is not the case. He says:

> By predestination we mean the eternal decree of God, by which He determined with Himself whatever He wished to happen with regard to every man. All are not created on equal terms, but some are preordained to eternal life, others to eternal damnation; and, accordingly, as each has been created for one or other of those ends, we say that he has been predestined to life or death.[48]

Created for Damnation

It must be stressed that Calvin actually believed that those who are eternally damned were created to be damned just as the saved were created to be saved. And while Calvin claims to know in one sense why God elects to save those He elects (i.e., to be merciful; for His pleasure), he denies knowing why (i.e., the reason behind the reason) it was His pleasure to damn those He created for damnation or to save those He created for salvation. Calvin continues:

> We say, then, that Scripture clearly proves this much, that God by His eternal and immutable counsel determined once and for all those whom it was His pleasure one day to admit to salvation, and those whom, on the other hand, it was His pleasure to doom to destruction. We maintain that His counsel, as regard the elect, is founded on His free mercy, without any respect to human worth, while those whom He dooms to destruction are excluded from access to life by a just

---

[48] Ibid., book 3, chap 21, sec 5, 206.

and blameless, but at the same time **incomprehensible** *judgment.*[49] *(Emphasis mine)*

Just Love It and Leave It Alone

If the damned were damned because they deserved to be, or because they refused God's gift of eternal life—assuming it was offered to them—that would be quite comprehensible. What Calvin is admitting is that he does not have a clue, and no clues are available to explain why some are going to be saved and others lost. While on one level he believes some are saved for all eternity and others are lost for all eternity—because this is what pleases God—on another level he does not know why God is pleased with this. To even ask such a question was to Calvin the height of arrogance. According to Calvin:

> *The subject of predestination, which itself is attended with considerable difficulty, rendered very perplexed, and hence perilous by human curiosity, which cannot be constrained from wandering into forbidden paths, and climbing to the clouds, determined if it can that none of the secret things of God shall remain unexplored. When we see many, some of them in other respects not bad men, everywhere rushing into this audacity and wickedness, it is necessary to remind them of the course of duty in this matter. First, then, when they inquire into predestination, let them remember that they are penetrating into the recesses of the divine wisdom, where he who rushes forward securely and confidently instead of satisfying his curiosity will enter an inextricable*

---

[49]   Ibid., book 3, chap 21, sec 7, 210-211.

labyrinth. For it is not right that man should with impunity pry into the things which the Lord has been pleased to conceal within Himself, and scan that sublime eternal wisdom which it is His pleasure that we should not apprehend but adore that therein also His perfections may appear.[50]

Thus to Calvin it is not only God's good pleasure to damn some as well as save some, but it is also His good pleasure that we not know—in the most basic sense—why. We are therefore to love ("adore") double predestination but are incapable of really understanding ("apprehend") it and should for the most part just accept it, teach it and then leave it alone.

The Question of Justice

Calvin often acknowledged that his view of election raised questions that he could not answer. In fact, based upon what he believed regarding predestination, Calvin seemed to concede that it did *appear* as though God were unjust in His dealings with the unelect. To escape this conclusion he simply appealed to information or factors "hidden" from us. In other words, if we knew what God knew we could reconcile Justice and the Calvinist view of Election. But since we do not have all the information needed, we simply must accept that these two concepts are not at odds—no matter how it may appear. Calvin's detractors were, of course, all too willing to remind him of the apparent conflict between his doctrine of Election and Justice. With such people in mind Calvin says:

---

[50]   Ibid., book 3, chap 21, sec 1, 203-204.

> *They again object, "Were not men
> predestined by the ordination of God to that
> corruption which is now held forth as the
> cause of condemnation? If so, when they
> perish in their corruption, they do nothing
> else than suffer punishment for that calamity,
> into which, by the predestination of God,
> Adam fell, and dragged all his posterity
> headlong with him. Is not He, therefore unjust
> in cruelly mocking His creatures?"[51]*

Man's Damnation, God's Pleasure?

Now this would be the perfect time for Calvin to
say that these people who characterized Calvinism
this way were misrepresenting it. However, he does
not do this precisely because they were exactly right
in their representation of Calvinism with regard to
election and reprobation. While he was not
admitting injustice on God's part he was conceding
the *apparent* injustice. This is why Calvin went on to
say:

> *I admit that by the will of God all of the sons
> of Adam fell into that state of wretchedness
> in which they are now involved; and this is
> just what I said at the first, that we must
> always return to the mere pleasure of the
> Divine will, the cause of which is hidden in
> Himself.[52]*

In other words, only God knows why.

Boettner affirms that:

> *The Reformed Faith has held to the existence
> of an eternal, divine decree which,
> antecedently to any difference or desert in*

---

51   Ibid., book 3, chap 23, sec 4, 228.

52   Ibid.

men themselves separates the human race into two portions and ordains one to everlasting life and the other to everlasting death.[53]

Lest there be any confusion as to what Boettner means by this, he goes on to say that men are:

Thus predestined and foreordained, (and) are particularly and unchangeably designed; and their number is so certain and definite that it cannot be either increased or decreased.[54]

Elsewhere Boettner says that:

*The doctrine of absolute Predestination of course logically holds that some are foreordained to death as truly as others are foreordained to life. The very terms "elect" and "election" imply the terms "non-elect" and "reprobation." When some are chosen out others are left not chosen. The high privileges and glorious destiny of the former are not shared with the latter. This, too, is of God. We believe that from all eternity God has intended to leave some of Adam's posterity in their sins, and that the decisive factor in the life of each is to be **found only in God's will**.*[55]

With special attention given to the fact that we do not and cannot know why some are chosen for salvation Jay Adams, in his booklet, *Counseling and*

---

[53]   Lorraine Boettner, *The Reformed Doctrine of Predestination*, 83.

[54]   Ibid., 84.

[55]   Lorraine Boettner, *The Reformed Doctrine of Predestination*, 104.

the Five Points of Calvinism, makes it as clear as possible. He says:

> *God has chosen some to be saved.... The choice was unconditional.... The choice was made **entirely within God**, out of His own good pleasure. The selection of some for eternal life was made on the basis of **unrevealed factors** known to God alone.*[56] *(emphasis mine)*

Sproul asks, "Why does God choose to save some...." He then says:

> *The only answer I can give to this question is that I don't know. I have no idea. Why God saves some but not all...I know that He does not choose to save all. I don't know why.*[57]

Finally, W.R. Godfrey, professor of Church History at Westminster Seminary in California, explains the Augustinian doctrine of predestination as follows:

> *The reason that some sinners are saved and others lost must be **in God**. It is according to **God's purpose**, His eternal decree, that some sinners are rescued and others are left in their sins. The foundation of this divine decree is simply **the good pleasure or will of God**.*[58] *(emphasis mine)*

---

[56]   Jay Adams, *Counseling and the Five Points of Calvinism*, (Presbyterian and Reformed Publishing Co. 1981) , 11.

[57]   R.C. Sproul, *Chosen by God*, 36,37.

[58]   W.R. Godfrey, "Predestination," *New Dictionary of Theology* (Downers Grove, IL, Inter-Varsity Press, 1988), 528.

Human Freedom vs. Predestination

It should be kept in mind that Augustinianism, as it relates to predestination, is for all practical purposes Calvinism. Sproul concedes that the Calvinist view of:

> *Predestination seems to cast a shadow on the very heart of human freedom. If God has decided our destinies from all eternity, (unconditionally) that strongly suggests that our free choices are but charades, empty exercises in predetermined placating. It is as though God wrote the script for us in concrete and we are merely carrying out His scenario.*[59]

Sproul also says that,

> *It was certainly loving of God to predestine the salvation of His people, those the Bible calls the "elect or chosen ones." It is the non-elect that are the problem. If some people are not elected unto salvation then it would seem that God is not all that loving toward them. For them it seems that it would have been more loving of God not to have allowed them to be born. That may indeed be the case.*[60]

Sproul makes a valiant attempt at trying to explain how the Calvinist view of predestination and the concept of free-will are not incompatible. In my opinion he fails as he must. If he were to limit himself to what scripture actually says about predestination and free-will (i.e., human responsibility) he would have no such problem. The

---

[59]   R.C. Sproul, *Chosen by God*, 51.

[60]   Ibid., 32.

fact is that the Calvinist has simply gone too far in his definition of predestination. He is thus trapped by that same definition.

For example, no amount of genius can reconcile a meaningful and biblical definition of "free-will" with Boettners' extreme assertion that God "...creates the very thoughts and intents of the soul."[61]

If God creates the thoughts and intentions of the reprobate, then God and not the reprobate is responsible for those thoughts and intentions. But this is a quagmire that even Calvin wanted (albeit unsuccessfully) to avoid.

---

[61]   Lorraine Boettner, *The Reformed Doctrine of Predestination*, 32.

III
Limited Atonement
Explained

Limited Atonement, sometimes referred to as definite or particular atonement, is the Calvinistic doctrine which says Christ died for some (i.e., the elect) and not for others (i.e., the unelect). Logically, since Calvinists believe that God only intended to save the elect, only the elect would need Christ to die for them.

Likewise, since Calvinists believe God never intended for many in the world (i.e., all the unelect) to be saved, they see no reason or purpose for Christ to die for them. Thus, what Christ did for the elect—providing the basis for salvation, including the propitiation for and forgiveness of sins—He did not do for the unelect; nor did He ever intend to.

Certain Specified Sinners

Steele and Thomas state this doctrine accordingly:

> *Christ's redeeming work was intended to save the elect only and actually secured salvation for them. His death was a substitutionary endurance of the penalty of*

*sin **in the place of certain specified sinners**. In addition to putting away the sins of His people, Christ's redemption secured everything necessary for their salvation, including faith which unites them to Him. The gift of faith is infallibly applied by the Spirit to all for whom Christ died, thereby guaranteeing their salvation.[62] (Emphasis mine)*

Elsewhere Steele and Thomas state:

All Calvinists agree that Christ's obedience and suffering were of infinite value, and that if God had so willed, the satisfaction rendered by Christ would have saved every member of the human race. It would have required no more obedience, nor any greater suffering for Christ to have secured salvation for every man, woman, and child who ever lived than it did for Him to secure salvation for the elect only. But He came into the world to represent and save only those given to Him by the Father. Thus Christ's saving work was limited in that it was designed to save some and not others, but it was not limited in value for it was of infinite worth and would have secured salvation for everyone if this had been God's intention.[63]

---

[62]   David N. Steele and Curtis C. Thomas, *The Five Points of Calvinism*, 17.

[63]   David N. Steele and Curtis C. Thomas, *The Five Points of Calvinism*, 39.

Boettner says that:

Christ died not for an unorderly mass, but for His people, His Bride, His Church.[64]

Elsewhere Boettner affirms that "Calvinists hold that in the intention and secret plan of God, Christ died for *the elect only...*"[65] (Emphasis mine) He goes on to explain:

That this doctrine necessarily follows from the doctrine of election. If from eternity God has planned to save one portion of the human race and not another, it seems to be a contradiction to say that...He sent His Son to die for those whom He had predetermined not to save, as truly as...He was sent to die for those whom He had chosen for salvation. These two doctrines must stand or fall together. We cannot logically accept the one and reject the other. If God has elected some and not others to eternal life, then plainly the primary purpose of Christ's work was to redeem the elect.[66]

Four Point Calvinists?

In fairness to the so-called four point Calvinists, it should be noted that many, who otherwise seem to embrace authentic Calvinism, do not buy into Limited Atonement. However, I must also admit that the logic of believing Christ died for those that He did not elect—considering the Calvinistic view of election—escapes me. But, as one four-pointer told me: "I must believe what Scripture teaches and

---

[64]   Lorraine Boettner, *The Reformed Doctrine of Predestination*, 157.

[65]   Ibid., 150.

[66]   Ibid., 151.

cannot be concerned about whether or not it fits my overall system of theology." I would of course agree, and add the other four points to the same category as the 3rd point, that is, the category of the unbiblical. It should also be noted that the debate and disagreement between four-pointers and five-pointers cannot be reduced to only a difference of interpretation of the 3rd point. Rather, four-pointers outright reject the 3rd point. However, when they do they contradict the other four points and make themselves inconsistent Calvinists.

IV
Irresistible Grace
Explained

According to Calvinism, the unregenerate elect *cannot* respond to the Gospel or appropriate by faith what Christ did for them on the cross. Therefore God must also make provision for the elect, give them a new and spiritual birth (regeneration), and then give the newly regenerate person the faith to appropriate that provision.

Steele and Thomas explain:

> *In addition to the outward general call to salvation which is made to everyone who hears the gospel, the Holy Spirit extends to the elect a special inward call that inevitably brings them to salvation. The external (which is made to all without distinction) can be, and often is, rejected; whereas the internal call (which is made only to the elect) cannot be rejected; it always results in conversion. By means of this special call, the Spirit irresistibly draws the sinner to Christ. He is not limited in His work of applying salvation by man's will, nor is He dependent upon man's cooperation for success. The Spirit graciously causes the elect sinner to cooperate, to*

*believe, to repent, to come freely and willingly to Christ. **God's grace, therefore, is invincible; it never fails to result in the salvation of those to whom it is extended.**[67] (Emphasis mine)*

Make Them an Offer They Can't *Accept*

For lack of a better expression, there is a kind of Divine tease—Calvinistically speaking—that occurs with regard to the unelect. That is, we (Christians) are commanded to "invite them in" but they cannot accept that invitation. It is like inviting everyone to take a breath of fresh air, knowing that many, though not knowing which ones, do not have lungs with which to breathe.

Steele and Thomas explain:

*The gospel invitation extends a call to salvation to everyone who hears its message. It invites all men without distinction to drink freely of the water of life and live. **It promises salvation to all who repent and believe.** But this outward general call, extended to the elect and unelect alike, will not bring sinners to Christ. Why? Because men are by nature dead in sin and are under its power. They are of themselves unable and unwilling to forsake their evil ways and to turn to Christ for mercy. Consequently, the unregenerate will not respo*~~~ *to the gospel call to repentance and faith.* *No amount of external threatening or promises will cause blind, deaf, dead, rebellious sinners to bow before Christ as Lord and to look to Him alone for salvation. Such*

---

[67] David N. Steele and Curtis C. Thomas, *The Five Points of Calvinism*, 18.

an act of faith and submission is contrary to the lost man's nature.[68] (emphasis mine)

The Rub

The rub is that while we are promising "salvation to *all* who repent and believe," we are supposed to know that many of them can't and are not supposed to repent and believe.

Boettner says that:

As the bird with a broken wing is "free" to fly but not able, so the natural man is free to come to God but not able.[69]

Some freedom!

From a thoroughly Calvinistic perspective—though I doubt many Calvinists wish to dwell on this point—just as no amount of preaching will *help* the unelect, no failure of Christians to reach out to the elect will *hinder* them from coming to Christ. Thus, while the Gospel is to be proclaimed, it is difficult to see why we should be all that concerned— Calvinistically speaking. After all, according to Calvinism, the elect will be saved, period. The unelect will be damned period. If faith and unbelief are ultimately and inevitably the result of election and reprobation respectively, how could our evangelistic efforts or failure to evangelize really matter?

---

[68] Ibid., 48.

[69] Lorraine Boettner, *The Reformed Doctrine of Predestination*, 62.

A Meaningless Call?

Now I do not want to suggest that all Calvinists concede or even see the logical implication of irresistible grace. Such is not the case. Nevertheless, in view of the Calvinists' definition of the general and non-efficacious call, how can a Calvinist still manage to believe it is a real and meaningful offer of salvation? This kind of theological and logical schizophrenia is not isolated to a few uneducated Calvinists on the fringe. No less a Calvinist luminary than A.A. Hodge seems to want to have it both ways. That is, on the one hand he clearly affirms that the death of Christ was on behalf of and intended to benefit the elect only. Thus he says:

> *We believe that Christ died with the intention of saving all (and only) those whom he actually does save.*[70]

Nevertheless, after stating in no uncertain terms his belief in limited or definite atonement, he goes on to say:

> *The question (of limited atonement) does not relate to the universal offer in perfect good faith of a saving interest, in Christ's work **on the condition of faith**.*[71] *(emphasis mine)*

A Valid Offer?

It is amazing that someone so obviously intelligent could fail to see the inconsistency of holding to both limited atonement and a meaningful universal call to salvation. If Christ did not die for the unelect, and if the unelect are not called

---

[70]   A.A. Hodge, *The Atonement* (Memphis, TN: Footstool Publishing, [reprinted] 1987), 357.

[71]   Ibid.

efficaciously, and if only those called efficaciously can respond to the gospel with saving faith, how could the offer of salvation to the unelect be in good faith?

Sproul explains that:

The Calvinist view of predestination teaches that God actively intervenes in the lives of the elect to make absolutely sure that they are saved.[72]

He then says:

*Of course the rest are invited to Christ and given the "**opportunity**" to be saved **if they want to**...*[73]

Putting the word *opportunity* in quotes and the words *if they want to* in italics is Sproul's way of nodding that he understands that these are just words without much meaning in light of what Calvinism teaches about unconditional election, irresistible grace, predestination, etc. Thus he is quick to add that:

Calvinism assumes that without the intervention (i.e., regeneration) of God no one will ever want Christ. Left to themselves (i.e., unelected, unregenerate, etc.), no one will ever choose Christ.[74]

Sproul also says:

*Fallen man is still **free to choose** what he desires, but because his desires are only wicked he lacks the moral ability to come to*

---

[72]   R.C. *Sproul, Chosen By God*, 34.

[73]   Ibid., 34.

[74]   Ibid., 34.

Christ. As long as he remains...unregenerate, he will never choose Christ.[75] *(emphasis mine)*

But certainly one so erudite as Sproul knows that:

1. If Grace is irresistible,

and if:

2. Grace is essential to salvation,

then it follows:

3. No saving grace is extended to the unelect.

Thus, Calvinists are in the rather awkward position of claiming to make a valid offer of salvation (to the unelect) on the "condition of faith" while denying the only provision (i.e., Christ's death) of salvation is for the unelect. Not only so, while they are saying God promises to save the unelect if they believe (i.e., the condition) they are also saying the unelect cannot possibly believe and meet that condition. To add insult to injury, they are claiming this is just the way God (from all eternity) wanted it to be.

---

[75]   Ibid., 75.

V
Perseverance of the Saints *Explained*

Sometimes referred to as Perseverance of God in the Saints, Perseverance of the Saints should not be confused with what many other Evangelicals refer to as the Doctrine of Eternal Security. Both affirm that once a person is saved, he will always be saved. They differ, however in one important respect. The more common doctrine of Eternal Security says that once a person is saved, he is saved *because he believes*, regardless of how he may behave thereafter. The Calvinistic doctrine of Perseverance says that one who does not persevere in faith—and to some extent in the expression of faith (practice)—proves he was never really saved in the first place.

According to Calvinism, as Election determines who will be regenerated, believe in Christ, repent, be saved, etc., so regeneration guarantees that the regenerate will persevere in faith, which—Calvinistically speaking—cannot be distinguished from practice. This does not mean that Calvinists do not believe the regenerate cannot have lapses in the practice of their faith, or that all who are regenerate will persevere with the same degree of enthusiasm or produce the same quality or quantity of spiritual fruit. However, if you are among the saved, you will live *as if you are saved*—to some degree—throughout most if not all of your life, according to Calvinism.

The Inevitability of Perseverance

If you ask about the Saint who fails to persevere or say you know a Christian who abandoned faith, you miss the 5th point. That is, a true believer *will not* fail to persevere because he *cannot* fail to persevere.

According to Steele and Thomas:

All who were chosen by God, redeemed by Christ, and given faith by the Spirit are eternally saved. They are kept in faith by the power of Almighty God and thus persevere to the end.[76]

The Westminster Confession states:

They whom God hath accepted in the Beloved, effectually called and sanctified by His Spirit, can neither totally fall nor finally fall away from the state of grace: but shall persevere therein to the end, and be eternally saved.[77]

Hanko explains:

By this, we mean that one continues in the **state of holiness and righteousness** *to which*

---

[76]   David N. Steele and Curtis C. Thomas, *The Five Points of Calvinism*, 18.

[77]   *The Westminster Confession of Faith*, chapter 19, sec. 1.

> *he has been elevated through the work of the Holy Spirit, and he continues in this state through all of his way through the valley of the shadow of death until he is brought finally to glory.*[78] *(emphasis mine)*

Concerning those saints who do temporarily backslide, Hoeksema says:

> *God preserves even in their falls the incorruptible seed of regeneration in them, by His Word and Spirit effectually renews them unto repentance...*[79]

That is, all those that are truly regenerate and fall into sin will repent of that sin thereby demonstrating they are truly regenerate.

Practical vs. Positional Holiness

It must be kept in mind that the 5th point does not so much refer to perseverance unto salvation—though this is implied—but perseverance in holiness. That is, it does not primarily refer to the position or standing of the regenerate—with regard to ultimate and eternal *glorification*—but rather to the present practice or state of the regenerate, with regard to daily *sanctification*. No matter how much of an allowance a Calvinist will suggest for sin in the life of the saint—which varies from Calvinist to Calvinist—all true Calvinists will think of Perseverance of the Saints as the saints persevering to some degree in practical (vs. positional) holiness as the necessary and inevitable proof of regeneration.

---

[78]   H. Hanko and H.C. Hoeksema and J. Van Baren, *The Five Points of Calvinism*, 85.

[79]   Herman Hoeksema, *Reformed Dogmatics*, 548.

Boice sums up the 5th point as follows:

The mark of true justification is a perseverance in righteousness—to the very end...[80]

---

[80]   John F. MacArthur, *The Gospel According to Jesus,* (Zondervan Publishing House, 1415 Lake Drive, S.E., Grand Rapids, Michigan 49506), page xii.

FIVE
COUNTER POINTS
TO
CALVINISM

Proceed With Caution

Now that we have considered the Five Points from a Calvinistic perspective, it is time to evaluate them in light of Scripture. As noted at the outset, I emphatically disagree with the main message of each of the Points because I believe all five points are in conflict with the clear teaching of Scripture. However, a word of caution seems in order. I have learned the hard way that it is much easier to win arguments than people.

What I mean by this is that embracing error, as with embracing truth, is not simply an objective intellectual matter. People are emotionally "attached" to what they believe. You can point by point show the fallacy of a position—and if you are not careful—unnecessarily alienate the very person you are trying to reach. We must "speak the truth" on this and all matters but we should do so "in love." That does not mean you can entirely avoid offending people when exposing error. I do not believe this is possible. But we should do all we can to be gracious in our dealing with our brothers and sisters that we disagree with, realizing that everyone is capable of falling into error. Believing the truth is not something we should boast about but something we should be grateful for. With this in mind, let us now examine the Five Points in light of God's Holy and Inerrant Word.

VI
Calvinistic Total Depravity
Refuted

By way of review, keep in mind that Calvinistic Depravity is not so much a matter of how depraved the unregenerate *are* or *behave*, but what Total Depravity has done to the unregenerate. Calvinistically speaking, it says he cannot believe the Gospel while in this state. Left to himself, I would agree that lost and sinful man is not naturally reaching out to God. I would even agree that without God's gracious help (i.e., the Father must draw, the Spirit must convict, etc.) the unregenerate would not come to Christ in faith.

Nevertheless, in light of Scripture, how can the Calvinist say that the unregenerate cannot believe the Gospel unless he first becomes regenerate? Calvinist scholar, John H. Gerstner, in his interpretation of John 1:12 and 13 says:

> *We must not get the notion that people come to Jesus, and as a result of that they are "born again"...Those who do come to Jesus are not therefore born again, but on the contrary indicate that they have been*

*born again. In other words, they are not born
again because they have come to Jesus but
they have come to Jesus because they have
been born again.*[81]

When Gerstner rejects the idea that we can
"come to Jesus" before we are born again, he is
denying that receiving Christ or believing in Christ
is possible before regeneration. Not only so, but he is
also saying that the Apostle John (in 1:12 and 13) is
teaching the exact opposite of what John appears to
be teaching. Nevertheless, this notion—which
Gerstner says we are not supposed to get from John
1:12,13—is the exact notion John gives us.

To use John 1:12,13 to prove that regeneration
must precede faith in Christ is like using a globe to
prove the earth is flat. No one coming to this
passage without a Calvinistic bias could interpret it
as does Gerstner. In fact, just the opposite is true.
Unless one is wearing Calvinist colored glasses, such
a Calvinistic interpretation of this passage (i.e.,
rebirth before faith in Christ) is very difficult if not
impossible to maintain. The Apostle John says:

Faith First

*...As many as received (Christ), to them He
gave the right to become children of God,
to those who believe in His name: who were
born, not of blood, nor of the will of the flesh,
nor of the will of man, but of God. (John
1:12,13, NKJ)*

Does it not seem almost too obvious that John is
telling his readers that receiving Christ, which he

---

[81]   John H. Gerstner, *A Predestination Primer* (Grand
Rapids, Michigan: Baker Book House), 9.

equates with believing in Christ, is the prerequisite to becoming a child of God or being born...of God?

However, the Calvinist latches on to the words "human decision" and claims that this proves that man has no say (i.e., *cannot* receive or believe) in the matter. But it seems very clear that John is using the words "natural descent," "human decision," and "human will" in contrast to the words "born...of God" to emphasize who the *receiver/believer* is directly getting this new life from. That is, when you are born again you are born of God.

*The first birth is physical and natural.

*The second birth is spiritual and super-natural.

*The first birth is caused by and is the result of human activity.

*The second birth is caused by and is the result of Divine Activity.

To say that God is the cause of that Birth (i.e., the one who directly gives that life) is not to say that there is no God ordained prerequisite to regeneration.

Condition vs. Consequence

To reduce this *condition* (i.e., receiving or believing in Christ) for rebirth to a mere *consequence* of rebirth not only reverses the obvious order in these verses, but it also flies in the face of what John says elsewhere in this book as well as what Peter says about how one comes to be born again. Let us first consider the reason John said he recorded the miracles found in his Gospel. He says:

These are written that you may believe that
Jesus is the Christ, the Son of God, and that
believing you may have life in His name.
(John 20:31)

Again the signs are recorded so we can:

1. Believe Jesus is the Christ, the Son of God.

Believing that Jesus is the Christ, the Son of God,
is so that we:

2. May have life in His name.

You Must Have Life to Get Life?

Every Evangelical believer would agree that life
in His name cannot come apart from the new birth.
That is, the new birth is the beginning of that life.

If we must believe Jesus is the Christ, the Son of
God to have life in His name, *how* can the Calvinist
maintain that the new birth must come before faith?
This would mean that life comes before birth. In
keeping with the Calvinist interpretation of John
1:12,13 and the implication of the Calvinist view of
Depravity, you would have to believe that you must
have life (i.e., be born again) so you can believe Jesus
is the Christ, the Son of God and thereby receive life
in His name.

In other words, you have to have the life to get
the life. But if you already have it, why would you
need to get it? I apologize if it sounds as though I am
being facetious. Please be assured that my motive is
not to make fun of anyone. However, I must admit
to feeling compelled to demonstrate the absurdity of
the Calvinist position on rebirth relative to faith. As
noted earlier, the Calvinist position is not only that

Rebirth must precede faith but rebirth must precede
the inward or efficacious call as well. However,
Steele and Thomas, in their commentary of Romans
8:29,30 say that God:

*Calls (the elect) (1) Outwardly by the gospel
& (2) Inwardly by His Spirit thus giving them
life and faith.*[82]

Life Before Birth?

But that very same life and faith is just what the
Calvinist says comes with the new birth. In fact that
is why, according to Calvinism, we must be born
again first. But if the inward call results in new life
and saving faith, then regeneration is "in effect" the
inward call. How then can the Calvinist say that
regeneration comes before the inward or effectual
call? Is the order only logical and not chronological?

Regardless of how a Calvinist tries to resolve
this dilemma, the Apostle Peter says that we have:

*...Been born again, not by corruptible seed
but incorruptible, through the word of God
which lives and abides forever.... Now this is
the word which was preached to you. (1
Peter 1:23, 25)*

Is it necessary for us to believe the Gospel
(through which we are born again) in order to be
born again, or must we be born again to believe the
Gospel as the Calvinist contends? It is clear from
what Peter says that the incorruptible seed precedes
rebirth. The question is this: is the seed—God's
Word in the form of the Gospel—received by faith

---

[82]   David N. Steele and Curtis C. Thomas, *Romans: An
         Interpretive Outline* (Philadelphia, Pa: The
         Presbyterian and Reformed Publishing Co., 1963), 70.

or without faith? If it is received by faith then faith is before and leads to regeneration.

Life Before Conception?

James Boice, like all other Calvinists, insists that faith must follow regeneration because of the total inability resulting from the Total Depravity of man. Nevertheless, in his interpretation of 1 Peter 1:23 he says:

> God **first** plants within our heart what we might call the ovum of faith.... **Second**, He sends forth the seed of His Word, which contains the divine life within it, to pierce the ovum of faith. The result is spiritual conception.[83](emphasis mine)

Although Boice is careful to point out that the faith that enables a person to receive the Word is given by God, he nonetheless places faith before "spiritual conception" (as a prerequisite to conception) which is before spiritual birth, which in turn is before saving faith. However, if Boice is right, then faith is before spiritual birth since it is before spiritual conception. Even Calvin says that:

> ...Christ confers upon us, and we obtain by faith, both free reconciliation and newness of life.[84]

Depending upon what Calvin had in mind when he referred to "newness of life" it just may be,

---

83   James Boice, *Foundations of the Christian Faith* [Revised Edition] (Downers Grove, IL: Inter-Varsity Press, 1986), 407.

84   John Calvin, *Institutes of the Christian Religion*, [book 3, Chap 3, sec.1], 509.

as noted earlier, that Calvin was not really a Calvinist regarding the 1st point.

That is, if newness of life refers to regeneration, then according Calvin, regeneration must follow from faith and not precede it. At this point it will be instructive to consider what Calvin had to say about the relationship of faith to repentance. According to Calvin:

> *That repentance not only always follows faith, but is produced by it, ought to be without controversy...*[85]

Calvin also said that:

> *Those who think that repentance precedes faith instead of flowing from, or being produced by it, as the fruit by the tree, have never understood it.*[86]

In one sense Calvin believed:

> *...Under the term repentance is comprehended the whole work of turning to God, of which not the least important part is faith...*[87]

Nevertheless, in the sense that he is referring to above, faith is first. What he means by repentance when he refers to the repentance that follows faith and that flows from faith is what he calls the

---

[85]   Ibid., 509.

[86]   Ibid., 510.

[87]   Ibid., 512.

"quickening of the spirit."[88] This he says involves a "transformation… in the soul itself."[89]

According to Sproul, Ephesians 2:1-10 represents:

…A predestinarian passage p a r excellence…[90]

He then goes on to say that:

This passage celebrates the newness of life that the Holy Spirit has created in us.[91]

Keep in mind that it is newness of life that is obtained by faith according Calvin.

Then, so that there is no misunderstanding, Sproul goes on to say that:

What is here (in Ephesians 2:1-10) called quickening or being made alive is what is elsewhere called rebirth or regeneration…the beginning of spiritual life.[92]

To recap, Calvin says that:

*Repentance flows from Faith.

*Repentance is newness of life and the quickening of the Spirit.

Sproul says that newness of life and quickening of the spirit are:

*Regeneration and the beginning of spiritual life.

---

88   Ibid., 515.
89   Ibid., 513.
90   R.C. Sproul, *Chosen By God*, 113.
91   Ibid., 113.
92   Ibid., 113.

Calvin also said that:

In one word, then, by repentance I understand regeneration, the only aim of which is to form in us anew the image of God, which was sullied and all but effaced by the transgression of Adam.[93]

How exactly Calvinists, such as Sproul, reconcile Calvin's contention that faith precedes repentance which he equates with regeneration, with their insistence that faith must follow regeneration, I am not quite sure. However, if Calvin's words can be taken to mean what they seem to mean, then Calvin would not therefore be considered authentically Calvinistic on this 1st point. Much more germane to this issue however, is what scripture has to say.

Everyone Who Believes

The Apostle Paul said he was:

Not ashamed of the gospel of Christ, for it is the power of God to salvation for everyone who believes. (Romans 1:16)

In Romans 10:13 he also declares: "Whoever *calls* upon the name of the Lord shall be saved." He then asks several very important questions that speak to the heart of this issue:

*How shall they call on Him in whom they have not **believed**? And how shall they believe in Him of whom they have not **heard**? And how shall they hear without a **preacher**? And how shall they preach unless they are **sent**?*

---

[93]   John Calvin, *Institutes of the Christian Religion*, 515.

He then answers these questions with the words: "How beautiful are the feet of those who preach the gospel of peace, Who bring glad tidings of good things!" In answering the most important 'how' question with regard to our present concern he says: *"So then faith comes by hearing and hearing by the word of God."*

If Calvinism were true, Paul should have said "How shall we believe unless we are born again?" Although the Calvinist says that Faith comes by regeneration, Paul says that:

1. Faith comes by hearing.

2. Hearing comes by the Word of God.

3. The Word of God comes when someone proclaims it.

4. Someone proclaims the Word of God when they are sent to do so.

Thus those who call upon the name of the Lord (and are thereby saved) call upon Him *in Faith*. They call upon Him in faith as a result of believing the Gospel preached to them. It is that simple.

No Choice!

By placing faith after regeneration, the Calvinist is removing from the lost the only way God has provided for them to avail themselves of the Grace of God. And of course, that is just what Calvinism as a system forces him to do. Many Calvinists will admit that they came to Christ (or at least thought they did) when they believed the gospel that someone proclaimed to them.

However, now they are telling unbelievers (or the evangelist) that they (the unbeliever) cannot come to Christ so easily. In fact they are saying that the unbeliever may not even be able to come to Christ at all (i.e., no election, no regeneration, no faith, no salvation). At a recent Harvest crusade some very hyper-Calvinist zealots showed up with T-shirts that had the word "choice" circled with a diagonal line through it indicating that you do not have a choice. They actively sought to discourage people from making a choice to accept Jesus Christ as Savior.

They are like men who safely and easily cross over a deep and dangerous canyon on the only bridge provided for that purpose. Then they tell others that there may not be a bridge (for them) to cross over on, and if there is, they will simply find it under them some day. How sad and tragic!

Faith Is the Answer to the Question-How?

While I believe John 1:12,13 makes it clear that a person is born again upon and as a result of believing in Jesus Christ, it is still helpful to consider the question asked by Nicodemus about *how* one can be born again. There are really two "how" questions that we could consider. That is, one could simply answer that it is what God does supernaturally.

It is God giving life and making us His Spiritual Children as a result. That, of course, does not really tell us how He does it. But it is enough for most of us to know *that* He does it. After all, God is omnipotent, and He has the power to do whatever He pleases. But from the perspective of the lost we might also ask *"how* can I make sure that I am one of those to whom God gives this new life or new birth?" The Calvinist would say there is nothing you can do to determine whether or not you will be born again.

In John 3:3 and 3:7, perhaps the most famous of all passages about rebirth, Jesus said to Nicodemus:

> *Most assuredly, I say unto you, unless one is born again, he cannot see the kingdom of God.*

A little later on in His conversation with Nicodemus He says:

> *Do not marvel that I said to you, "you must be born again."*

The Calvinist would have us believe that our Lord was only telling Nicodemus what *must* happen if you are to see or enter the kingdom. He was not, according to Calvinism, telling Nicodemus that he *ought* to be born again as if Nicodemus had a say in the matter.

The Calvinistic *must* is the inevitable result of election.

However, even to the most careless student it should be obvious that Jesus is still talking to Nicodemus when in John 3:16 He says:

> *For God so loved the world that He gave His only begotten Son, that whoever believes in Him should not perish but have everlasting life.*

John 3:16 Says it All

I submit that John 3:16 is the answer to Nicodemus' question of "How" one can be born again-both in terms of the *cause* (God) and *condition* (Faith). Jesus, in this most beloved of all verses, says:

1. How God feels about the world (i.e., loves it).

2. The extent to which He loves it, (i.e., gave His Son for it).

3. What He offers to the world through His Son (i.e., eternal life).

4. How *anyone* can receive what He offers *everyone* (i.e., whoever believes).

Remember that the context of John 3:16 is the context of John 3:3 and 3:7. Our Lord did not say what He said (recorded in chapter 3 verse 16) of this Gospel in a vacuum. He said it in the context of a conversation with Nicodemus about the absolute necessity of regeneration.

Thus, what our Lord told Nicodemus *must* happen, He was also saying that it *ought* to happen; and what ought to happen *can* happen. Thus, rebirth is not only *caused* by God it is *commanded* by God. God causes it to happen when we meet the God ordained condition for it to happen. That is, when we believe in or receive Jesus Christ.

But the Calvinist asks, how can a person spiritually dead, make a spiritual decision (i.e., believe in or receive Christ)?

Boettner reasons as follows:

If a man were dead, in a natural and physical sense, it would at once be readily

> *granted that there is no further possibility of that man being able to perform any physical actions. A corpse cannot act in any way whatever, and that man would be reckoned to have taken leave of his senses who asserted that it could. If a man is dead spiritually, therefore, it is surely equally as evident that he is unable to perform any spiritual actions.*[94]

Although there is a valid analogy between spiritual birth and physical birth and between spiritual death and physical death, the Calvinist goes too far in comparing them. For example, just because there is a physical gestation period of nine months between physical conception and physical birth, do we conclude that there is a corresponding spiritual gestation period? Likewise just because a person is spiritually dead does not mean he cannot believe the gospel when it is presented to him. In fact, since it is only to the lost (i.e., the spiritually dead) the gospel is preached it should be assumed (and Scripture does) that he can.

Calvinists are "stuck" with scriptures that make it clear that someone is suppose to believe in order to be saved. While they admit that the command to believe is to be directed at the unregenerate, they also deny that the unregenerate can obey the command as an unregenerate. Thus they say the unregenerated elect are regenerated so they will believe. However believing for the regenerate, in Calvinism, is not a command to obey but a gift that

---

[94]   Lorraine Boettner, *The Reformed Doctrine of Predestination*, 66.

is involuntarily received. After all, how can a *dead man* believe?

When they say the elect are regenerated so they *can* believe, they mean the elect are regenerated and *will* believe. The Calvinist also (intentional or otherwise) makes a distinction between the faith that is received involuntarily as a gift with or as the result of regeneration and the exercise of that faith (i.e., faith in Christ). Allow me to illustrate.

Suppose I wanted to turn a poor man into a rich man. I could offer him money which he could refuse and thereby remain poor. Or I could simply put the money in his bank account (or pocket). Now suppose that before this man becomes rich (i.e., before I give him the money) I tell him that he must accept the money I offer him. In the latter case, it is possible to say that he *received* the money that I put in his pocket but it is not possible to say that he accepted the money he received.

The Calvinist wants to have it both ways. He wants to say that faith is a gift that comes with regeneration. He also wants to say that after the person is regenerate he exercises his newly freed or revived will to believe in Jesus Christ and be saved. In other words, he believes God causes the elect lost to receive regeneration (which comes with faith) involuntarily so that he can voluntarily accept all that is available to him and that is his through faith. Thus we have an involuntarily received faith, followed by a voluntarily exercised faith to accept all that comes to us through that faith.

But that would mean that there is gift of faith that is not equal to believing in Christ. In other words, as money must be spent so faith must be exercised. But can biblical faith, which is also a saving faith, be viewed as anything less than or short of faith *in* Jesus Christ? If the Calvinist says that the faith we are given is faith *in* Jesus Christ, it would be like putting money in a man's pocket and spending it for him at the same time. But if the one who gives us the faith gives us an exercised faith (i.e., a faith in Christ) then it is not the newly regenerated that is doing the believing but God. That in turn would mean that saving faith is God believing in His Son through us. Sound ridiculous? It is.

Again all this just tends to complicate, distort and confuse what is in Scripture a very straightforward proposition. That is:

*Before we become Christians we are lost in our sins and in need of a savior. Jesus Christ died on the cross to save us from our sins and then triumphed over death. We simply need to turn to Him in faith. He then saves us. Sound simple? It is.

Can the Unregenerate Repent?

And if unregenerate man (i.e., the lost) cannot repent, why would God command him to do so? Paul tells us that "now [God] commands all men everywhere to repent" (Acts 17:30). Is it really possible, as the Calvinist would have us believe, that God does not really intend for any of the unelect to repent; that He was commanding them to do what He knew they were incapable of doing?

Conversely are we supposed to believe that He was commanding the elect to do what they could not help but do? This would be like commanding rain from cloudless skies (unelect) and from clouds filled with moisture (elect). In both cases you would be wasting your words. In the first case the commandment is meaningless because it cannot happen. In the second instance the commandment is meaningless because it would happen anyway.

Why Do the Lost Perish?

In light of the 1st point, it would also seem reasonable to ask why Paul would say concerning those ultimately lost, "They perish because *they refused to love the truth and so be saved*" (2 Thess. 2:10). The Calvinist would have us believe that this refusal is involuntary and inevitable. However, that which is involuntary and inevitable cannot be refused. By definition, something refused must be voluntary and not inevitable.

Scripture uses the language of responsibility and culpability. God wants you to know what you *must do* to be born again (i.e., believe), as opposed to what you *will do because* you are born again. The well known Calvinist Pastor and writer, Dr. D. James Kennedy seems to concede this very point. In his book, *Why I Believe*, in a chapter stressing the necessity of rebirth, he says:

> We have an imperative, that is true, but it contains within itself the germ of a promise. For if it is true that we must be born again, then it is also true that we **may** be born again...We can be forgiven. We can be recreated. We can have new hearts, new affections, new life, new power, new

*purpose, new direction, new destinations.
Yes we **may** be born again. That my friends is
the **good news**.*[95]

Dr. Kennedy even seems to concede that faith
comes before and results in regeneration when he
says to his readers:

*Place your trust in (Christ). Ask Him to come in
and be born in you today.*[96]

Calvinism therefore has its theological cart
before the biblical horse. Thus to accept the 1st point
of Calvinism is to reject—no matter how
unwittingly— a reasonable interpretation of John
3:16 as well as many other portions of Scripture.

---

[95]   James D. Kennedy, *Why I believe* (Dallas, Texas:
         Word Publishing, 1980), 138.

[96]   Ibid., 140.

VII
Unconditional Election
Refuted

If, as the Calvinist contends, God has elected only some to salvation, unconditionally, and others He leaves to damnation without recourse, having no interest in seeing them saved, why does Paul tell Timothy that God: "desires all men to be saved and to come to the knowledge of the truth" (1 Tim. 2:4). If Calvinism is correct "all men" should be "all elect men" or perhaps all kinds of men (i.e., some black, white, Jewish, Gentile, Russian, American, etc.).

The only other Calvinistic alternative is to say that God desires to save all men, but for reasons unknown did not elect (or send His Son to die for) most of those He desired to save, thereby derailing His own desire to save them. Would it not be better as well as more sensible and biblical, to simply agree with Paul and say "God desires all men to be saved?"

And why does Peter say that:

*The Lord...is longsuffering toward us, not willing that **any** should perish but that all should come to repentance. (2 Peter 3:9)*

If Calvinism is right then this should read that God does not want *any* of the *elect* to perish. Otherwise it would mean that He determined (with regard to the unelect) contrary to what He wanted. It would also mean that God takes pleasure in what He does not want.

In keeping with Calvinism, and with 2 Peter 3:9 in mind, Sproul asks:

*How can we square this verse with (the Calvinist view of) predestination?...What is the antecedent to **any**?[97] (emphasis his)*

Sproul then answers that:

It is clearly us...I think that what he is saying here is that God does not will that any of us (the elect) perish.[98]

Thus the Calvinist view is simply saying that the delay is only due to the fact that those who were elected to salvation from eternity have not all been saved yet in time. In other words, God is not longsuffering so that the lost *may* turn in faith to Christ and be saved, but because the elect lost, who *will* turn in faith to Christ because they are elect, need the time to do this. Thus God must be longsuffering to give the elect the time to do what He determined they will do.

---

[97]   R.C. Sproul., *Chosen by God*, 195, 197.

[98]   Ibid., 197.

A *Calvinistic* John 3:16

Calvinistically speaking, we can accurately paraphrase and amplify John 3:16 to read:

> *"For God so loved the **elect** of the world only, that He gave His only begotten Son, that whosoever of the **elect** that believes in Him—by which I mean all of the elect, who in fact believe because they are the elect, and cannot do otherwise—will not perish but have everlasting life."*

As silly as this sounds it is exactly what Calvinistic Election leads to.

Jesus tells us that no one knows "The Father except the Son, and He to whom the Son *wills* to reveal Him." Calvinists use statements such as this as a proof-text for their view of election. They point to the word "wills" and say "those that may know God are determined by God and His will and not a matter that we have a say in." However if you continue reading, our Lord identifies those to whom He "wills" to reveal the Father. With obvious compassion He says:

> *Come unto Me **all** you who labor and are heavy laden, and I will give you rest. (Matthew 11:27-30)*

Are we supposed to believe that *only* the elect lost "labor and are heavy laden"? We only have two choices here.

1. Calvinism

a. Christ was inviting all who labor and are heavy laden.

b. Only the elect (while lost) labor and are heavy laden.

2. Scripture

a. Christ was inviting all who labor and are heavy laden.

b. All the lost labor and are heavy laden.

The Kingdom of Heaven is Like....

While Calvinism is in search of the elect few who will come to Christ regardless of any effort to reach them, our Lord appealed to the troubled many (all sinners) and asked them to make a decision, or as Billy Graham might say, "take a step of faith" (i.e., come to Me).

Jesus said:

*The kingdom of heaven is like a certain king who arranged a marriage for his son, and set out for his servants to call those who were invited to the wedding; and **they were not willing to come.** Again, he sent out other servants, saying, "Tell those who are invited, see, I have prepared my dinner; my oxen and fatted cattle are killed, and all things are ready. Come to the wedding." But they made light of it and went their ways, one to his own farm, another to his business. And the rest seized his servants, treated them spitefully, and killed them. But when the king heard about it, he was furious. And he sent out his armies, destroyed those murderers, and burned up their city. Then he said to his servants, "The wedding is ready, but those who were invited were not worthy. Therefore go into the highways, and as many as you find, invite to the wedding." So those servants went out into the highways and gathered* *together all whom they found, both bad and good. And the wedding hall was filled with guests. But when the king came in to see the guests, he saw a man there who did not have on a wedding garment. So he said to him, "Friend how did you come in here without a wedding garment?" And he was speechless. Then the king said to the servants, "Bind him hand and foot, take him away, and cast him into outer darkness; there will be weeping and gnashing of teeth." For many are called but few are chosen. (Matthew 22:2-14)*

Why Are Some Excluded/Included?

Concerning those "not willing to come," were they not willing to come, as Calvinism teaches, because they were not "chosen" or were they not chosen because they were not willing to come as Jesus seems to teach? And what about those who accepted the invitation and put on the proper apparel? Did they do so because they were chosen or were they chosen because they did so? It seems to me that you cannot agree with Jesus and at the same time logically embrace the 2nd point of Calvinism.

VIII
Limited Atonement
Refuted

If Christ died for the elect only, why does Paul tell Timothy:

> ...*there is one God and one Mediator between God and man, the man Christ Jesus, who gave Himself as a ransom for **all** men...* (1 Timothy 2:5)

Should this read "a ransom for all *the Elect* men"?

If Christ did not die for everyone, why would the writer to the Hebrews say of Christ that He: "suffered death, so that by the grace of God He might taste death for *everyone*"? (Hebrews 2:10)

Should this read "taste death for everyone *who is Elect*"?

If Christ did not die for those ultimately lost as well as those ultimately saved, who is Peter referring to when he refers to those that were: "denying the Lord that bought them."

If Calvinists are right about perseverance, they cannot be backslidden Christians. If Calvinists are right about limited atonement, Christ could not have died for them.

If He "bought them," what price did He pay for them? If the price He paid was not the basis for salvation, then what? Did Christ pay one price for the elect (by dying on the cross) and another for the unelect?

And what does the Apostle John mean when he says, Jesus:

> *is...the atoning sacrifice for our sins, and not only for ours but also for the Sins of the **whole world**. (1 John 2:2)*

Did he really mean and should he have said, "also for the sins of the whole world of the elect"?

Drawing his listener's attention to the person of Jesus Christ, John the Baptist said, "Behold! The Lamb of God who takes away the sin of the world" (John 1:29).

A Calvinist reading of this verse could be "Behold! The Lamb of God who takes away the sin *of the elect* of the world."

The Apostle Paul tells us that "God was in Christ reconciling the world to Himself" (2 Corinthians 5:19).

If the Calvinist is right, this should be rendered "God was in Christ reconciling *the elect* of the world to Himself."

It was the position of the Apostle John that "The Father has sent the Son as the Savior of the world" (1 John 4:14).

A Calvinistically corrected reading would be "The Father has sent the Son as the Savior of *the elect* of the world."

Paul also tells us that "Christ died for the ungodly" (Romans 5:6).

To be consistent with Calvinism, Paul should have said that "Christ died *only for the ungodly elect.*"

What Does God Desire?

Perhaps one of the most difficult (I believe impossible) passages of Scripture for a Calvinist to reconcile with limited atonement is 1 Timothy 2:1 and 2. It is there that we read that:

...God our Savior...desires all men to be saved and to come to the knowledge of the truth.

Just a few verses earlier Paul wrote:

This is a faithful saying and worthy of all acceptance, that Christ Jesus came into the world to save sinners....

I take this to mean that if you are a sinner, He came to save you. However, the reason Paul can say with such confidence that God desires to save all men and to have all men come to the knowledge of the truth is even more devastating to the notion of limited atonement. That is, he can say this because:

There is one God and one Mediator between God and Men, the Man Christ

*Jesus, who gave Himself for all... (1 Timothy
2:5,6).*

Notice that Paul says that Christ, the only
Mediator, mediated for all. That is, if as every
Calvinist would agree, Christ did His mediating
work on the cross, then it follows that what He did
on the cross (i.e., die a substitutionary death for our
sins) He did for all sinners. Notice also that this
teaching about our Lord's mediating work, which
paid the ransom for all, is mentioned immediately
after Paul tells us about God's desire to save all men.
How could God's intentions toward all sinners be
stated more clearly? How could the Calvinist not see
this?

Good News/Bad News?

In effect, the 2nd point of Calvinism has turned
the Gospel (or good news of salvation) into
something like one of those not so funny *good
news/bad news* jokes.

As a result, a consistent Calvinistic
"evangelistic" proclamation could go something like
this:

*The good news is that if you are in the world
and a sinner, Jesus said He came to take
away the sin of the world. The bad news is
that perhaps He did not have your sins in
mind.*

*The good news is that if you are in the world,
Jesus came to be the savior of the world. The
bad news is that you may not be one of
those in the world He came to save.*

*The good news is that if you are unjust, Jesus
died for the unjust. The bad news is that you
might not be one of the unjust He died for.*

And, of course, if the Calvinist is right, you will simply be stuck *for* all eternity with the bad news because you have been stuck *from* all eternity with the bad news.

Seeking to Save the Lost

Jesus, referring to Himself and His purpose for coming, said that "The Son of Man has come to seek and save that which was lost." (Luke 19:10)

Calvinistically speaking, it would be more precise if not more accurate to say that "The Son of Man has come to seek and save *the lost elect*."

In his now classic sermon entitled "GOOD NEWS For The Lost," Charles Spurgeon ministered to the unsaved attending one of his services as follows:

> *I would have all anxious hearts consider HOW THE OBJECTS OF MERCY ARE HERE DESCRIBED: "The Son of Man is come to seek and save that which was lost." I feel inexpressibly grateful for this description– "that which was lost!" There cannot be a case so bad as not to be comprehended in this word "lost." I am quite unable to imagine the condition of any man or woman so miserable as not to be contained within the circumference of these four letters– lost.*[99]*(capitalization his)*

Spurgeon went on to exhort the lost in his listening audience with these very encouraging and un-calvinistic words:

---

[99]   Charles Spurgeon, *Good News for the Lost*.

Dear friends, "The Son of Man is come to seek and to save that which was lost." Does not the description suit you? Are you not among the lost? Well then, you are among such as Jesus Christ came to save. [100]

How Spurgeon was able to reconcile his view of Unconditional Election and Limited Atonement with the above statement I do not know. Nevertheless, he was exactly right regarding our Lord's interest in the lost. In this sermon he seemed to fully grasp the significance of our Lord's teaching on this vital matter. However, and unfortunately, I cannot say the same for Calvinism in general, or the 3rd point of Calvinism in particular.

The gospel is indeed good news for the lost. Not some of the lost, but all of the lost. The fact that some of the lost refuse to believe the good news and thereby forfeit the benefit and blessing which could otherwise be theirs is for that reason all the more tragic. Even the Calvinist must concede that unbelievers are addressed in scripture in a way that makes unbelief seem avoidable and self-imposed.

If, on the other hand, Christ did not die for some of the lost, (i.e., the unelect) then He certainly did not come to seek and to save them. If He did not come to seek and to save them, it is hard to imagine anything good (for them anyway) about the news proclaimed to them. If the 3rd point is correct, Spurgeon should have titled his sermon, "Good News for Some of the Lost." Or perhaps "Good News for the Elect Lost."

---

[100]   Ibid.

If Jesus only died for some of the lost, it is also certain that He did not come to seek and to save those He did not die for. If He did not come to seek and to save you, where is the good (for you) in the news? If Calvinism is right then the Gospel is only the Gospel (i.e., Good News) when it is preached to the elect. But even Calvinists claim that it is *good news* or the Gospel they are told to proclaim to all the lost. Thus, a consistent Calvinism is difficult if not impossible to maintain.

Breaking Rank

As noted earlier, the 3rd point is so obviously unscriptural that many Calvinists break rank with Calvinism and call themselves four-pointers. I agree with Packer and others when they say that consistency demands that the one who embraces the other four points should also accept the 3rd point. But I can also sympathize with four-pointers who see no way around (scripturally speaking) the unlimited provision for salvation offered to all through faith in Christ's death on the cross.

IX
Irresistible Grace
Refuted

It is true that if something is earned or merited, it is not truly of Grace. If you have to work for it, it is not really a gift - but a wage. But a gift that is received by the one to whom it is offered is no less a gift because the recipient voluntarily accepts it. I mention this because I occasionally hear Calvinists say that if we have a choice or use our will to accept God's gift of Eternal Life that this would somehow make the gift not a gift. Calvinists go further by stating that even if the unregenerate were willing, he would not be able to receive the gift offered to him. Hoeksema says:

> *...It is alleged (that) faith is the hand by which we take hold of the proffered salvation, the salvation proffered in the gospel...this is not true...the natural man has no hand whereby he is able to accept the salvation of God in Christ Jesus.*[101]

---

[101] Herman Hoeksema, *Reformed Dogmatics*, 479.

Which is to say that according to Calvinism, the natural man cannot have faith through which he might be saved. This however, is like saying to a man without a hand, "Please, reach out with your hand, and take this gift." If you or I were to do this, knowing the man had no hand, we would be considered very cruel indeed. We would be mocking the handless man. But isn't this just what the Calvinist is saying about God? That is, according to Calvinism, God is offering the unelect, natural man salvation on "the condition of faith" knowing full well that the unelect, natural man does not have and cannot have faith.

Can Grace Be Resisted?

The question before us however, is this; can grace be resisted and is grace ever resisted insofar as salvation is concerned? The only scriptural answer is *yes*. And just as a gift voluntarily received is no less a gift, so a gift "willfully refused" is no less a gift. The nature of the offer (i.e., free) is not affected by the intended recipient's response.

We have already read where Paul said that certain people perish because they *refuse* to love the Truth.

If we are to take Calvinism seriously, we must conclude that this is an "involuntary refusal." Can there be such a thing? Some Calvinists would contend that the unregenerate can choose evil, but evil only. But this is like saying the blind man can only choose not to see. Some choice. In fact, the blind do not choose not to see, they have no choice in the matter. So the unregenerate according to

Calvinism does not really choose to refuse, he simply does the only thing he can - *refuse*.

When you do the only thing you can and must do, that is not really a choice at all. The truth is that an *involuntary refusal* is an oxymoron. According to Calvinism, we can no more blame the unelect for being lost than we can legitimately blame a man born blind for his blindness. If a blind man was offered a cure for his blindness and refused this cure we could legitimately say that it is his fault that he remains blind. However, if a man is born blind, and cannot do anything about his blindness, how can we blame him for not seeing?

Is God Teasing the Unelect?

This is, in effect, what Calvinists are saying to the unregenerate unelect; you are born depraved, can do nothing about your depravity, and God who could does not want to and will not do anything about it.

From the point of view of the Evangelist, this is also like saying to the blind, I promise you eyesight on the condition you can "see" all the colors of the rainbow first. But, knowing full well your blindness does not allow you to see at all, the Evangelist just goes through the motions and makes empty promises since he can't distinguish the elect blind from the unelect blind.

If we extend this analogy to the unregenerate elect, it is like "saying they are born blind, but God will give them sight." Translated, if you are elect, you will be saved and have no meaningful say in the matter. Grace cannot be resisted. But, if this is so, why do the Apostles seem so intense in their effort to get the unbeliever to believe?

Again, if the elect "will" regardless and the unelect "can't" regardless, are we not really wasting words - or at best just going through the motions? If the elect must and the unelect can't, are we (i.e., those of us who proclaim the good news) just posturing? It makes no sense to command someone to do what they can't do (i.e., repent, believe) or what they cannot help but do (i.e., repent and believe). But, as we have already read, God commands all men everywhere to repent. If grace is irresistible for the elect and only an illusion or tease for the unelect, it would all appear to be just a game of infinite cruelty and consequence.

Caught Resisting Grace?

With all this in mind, let us consider just a few of the appeals made by Scripture in general and our Lord in particular to what sometimes seems like resisting souls.

To the entire city of Jerusalem our Lord says:

*Oh Jerusalem, Jerusalem...how often I wanted to gather your children together, the way a hen gathers her chicks under her wings, and **you were unwilling**. (Matthew 23:37)*

Could He have just as easily have said they "were unable"? And if they were unwilling only because they were unable, their unwillingness is not a matter of choice, but a matter of having no choice. Could it be that Christ was sad not because they were unwilling but because they were unelect? For had they been elected, they could not have been unwilling according to Calvinism since grace is irresistible.

Saving Faith

And what of the Philippian Jailer? In desperation he asked, "What must I do to be saved?" Paul answered him, "Believe on the Lord Jesus Christ, and you will be saved" (Acts 16:30,31).

What if Paul said you must first be among the elect, then you will not be able to resist the grace that saves. And if you are among the elect, unable to resist the grace that saves, you will believe on the Lord Jesus Christ as proof that you are not resisting the Grace and are one of the elect. Conversely, he could have said,

If you are not elected you cannot do anything to be saved because God does not want to save you, etc., etc.

Before Paul was finished, the suicidal jailer would probably have killed himself out of confusion if not despair.

And what are we to make of Stephen's words to the crowd who eventually stoned him:

You men who are stiff-necked and uncircumcised in heart and ears are always resisting the Holy Spirit.

Is it possible to resist the Holy Spirit and not the grace He administers?

If grace cannot be resisted —and if some unregenerate are not offered grace— to whom is the writer to the Hebrews referring when using these words; "Today if you hear His voice, do not harden your heart?" (Hebrews 4:6) They must either be elect or unelect. Is there any other category? If grace is irresistible for the elect (and these are the elect), how could they harden their hearts and why would they need to be warned not to do so?

Likewise, if grace is not extended to the unelect (and these are the unelect), how could they do anything else and why would they be warned not to do so?

However, to the woman at the well Jesus said:

If you knew the gift of God, and who it is who says to you give Me a drink, you would have asked Him, and He would have given you living water. (John 4:10)

In this context it is clear that the living water to which Jesus referred is the salvation which comes (as the Calvinist would agree) by grace. For Jesus also said:

Whoever drinks of this (well) water will thirst again. But whoever drinks of the water that I shall give him will never thirst. But the water that I shall give him will become in him a fountain of water springing up into everlasting life. (John 4:13,14)

For the Asking

Yet Jesus said it was hers *for the asking* if only she knew who He was and what He was offering. And how could she know who He was and what He was offering? He could tell her. And that is, of course, just what He did. She in turn went to town in what turned out to be an evangelistic endeavor. After she got the town's people interested in Jesus, by raising the possibility that Jesus could be the Messiah, we are told that:

> *Many of the Samaritans of that city believed in Him because of the word of the woman who testified, "He told me all things that ever I did." So when the Samaritans had come to Him, they urged Him to stay with them; and He stayed there two days. And many more believed because of His own word. Then they said to the woman, "Now we believe, not because of what you said, for we have heard for ourselves and know that this is indeed the Christ, the Savior of the world."* (John 4:39-42)

However, in John, chapter 6, there are several statements made by Christ, that when taken out of context, seem to support the Calvinistic contention that grace is irresistible. They are:

> **All that the Father gives Me will come to Me.*
>
> **This is the will of the Father who sent Me, that all that the Father has given Me I should lose nothing.*
>
> **No one can come to Me except the One who sent Me draws him.*

However, as soon as you put these words into their biblical context, a Calvinistic interpretation seems forced at best.

In verse 35 and 36 of John, chapter 6, Jesus says:

> *I am the bread of life. He who comes to Me shall never hunger, and He who believes in Me shall never thirst. But I said to you (those that were opposing Him) that you have seen Me and yet have not believed.*

In other words, the reason they did not come to Him is because they did not believe. It is in this context that Jesus says:

*All that the Father gives Me will come to Me
and I will by no means cast out.*

Neither Rejected Nor Ejected

That is, those that believe in Him are one and
the same as those that the Father gives to Him. By
coming to Christ in faith, the sinner can be assured
that he will not be rejected nor ejected from the
Kingdom of God. He is making the lost aware of
how secure in Christ they will be if they will come to
Christ in Faith. He is also making the saved aware of
how secure in Christ they are because they have
come to Christ in Faith. To further demonstrate that
this is indeed our Lord's purpose, consider the next
two verses.

> *For I have come down from heaven, not to
> do My own will, but the will of Him who sent
> Me. This is the will of the Father who sent Me,
> that of all that He has given Me I should lose
> nothing, but should raise it up at the last day.*

Once again, the context makes it evident that the
ones given to the Son by the Father are the ones who
come to Christ in Faith. For in the next verse He
says:

> *This is the will of Him who sent Me, that
> everyone who sees the Son and believes in
> Him may have everlasting life; and I will raise
> him up at the last day.*

Again, while speaking to those that opposed
Him, He said:

> *There are some of you who do not
> believe...Therefore I have said to you that no
> one can come to Me unless it has been
> granted to him by My Father.*

That is, those that believe are given to the Son and those that do not believe are not given to the Son. You must therefore come to Christ in Faith or you cannot come to Christ at all. But if you do come to Christ in Faith you will neither be rejected nor ejected.

At this point the Calvinist is likely to ask "How is it that a lost and depraved (one spiritually dead) sinner is able to come to Christ?" By God's grace and with God's help—that's how.

The Father Draws

The fact that God offers just such help is to be found in the very context that we are now considering. That is, Jesus said:

> *No one can come to Me unless the Father draws him; and I will raise him up at the last day. (John 6:44)*

Exactly what He does to draw us we are not told in this passage. Perhaps John 16:8 holds the answer. There we are told by Jesus that,

> *When the Holy Spirit has come, He will convict the world of sin, and of righteousness, and of judgment.*

Whatever this convicting work of the Holy Spirit is, it is a work the Holy Spirit does in the life of those *in the world*— not the church. Our Lord had the lost in mind, not the saved.

But why do some positively respond when God draws them? The Calvinist argues that everyone who is drawn cannot help but respond positively. In fact, Sproul appealing to Kittels' Theological Dictionary of the New Testament argues that the

word translated draw (elko) means to coerce, force
or even drag. He notes that in James 6:2 the same
word is translated drag. That is:

> *"Do not the rich oppress you and **drag** you
> into the courts?" He also points out that in
> Acts 16:19 the past tense of this word is
> translated **"dragged."**[102]*

> *When her masters saw that their hope of
> profit was gone, they seized Paul and Silas
> and **dragged** them into the marketplace to
> the authorities.*

What he does not say is that a form of this same
word is also used in John 12:32 where we read:

> *If I am lifted up from the earth, I will **draw** all
> men to Myself.*

While the New King James version uses the
word *peoples* instead of *men*, the word is supplied
by the translators. Actually it could be translated "If
I be lifted up from the earth, I will draw all (or
everyone) to Myself." Thus if the *drawing* of John
6:44 (i.e., by the Father) can be translated forced,
coerced or dragged, could we not say the same for
the drawing of John 12:32 (by and to the Son). This
would of course lead to universalism (i.e., everyone
will be saved) which Calvinists rightly reject. The
only other Calvinistic option would be to
paraphrase this verse as follows:

"If I be lifted up from this earth I will draw all
elect men unto Myself" or "If I be lifted up from the
earth I will draw all kinds of men (i.e., from different
nations) to Myself."

---

[102]   R.C. Sproul, *Chosen by God*, 186.

However, as Sproul surely knows, a single Greek word (such as elko) can be used to convey very different ideas depending upon the context. This is, in fact, why the translators of most translations used different English words (i.e., draw, drag) to translate what is essentially the same Greek word. Nevertheless, as interesting as all this might be to some, it really misses the point of the greater context.

Not Willing

If we move on just a little further in the narrative of John's gospel, we read where Jesus addressed His opponents as follows:

> *You do not have the (Father's) Word abiding in you, **because** whom He sent, Him you do not believe. You search the Scriptures, for in them you think you have eternal life; and these are they that testify of Me. But you are **not willing to come to Me** that you may have life. (John 5:38-40)*

The difference between the saved and the lost is the difference between Faith and Unbelief. The difference between those merely convicted by the Holy Spirit, and those who yield to the Spirit when they are drawn, is the difference between the willing and the unwilling. Thus, the 4th point of Calvinism misses the whole point.

X
Calvinistic Perseverance of the Saints
Refuted

It is certainly true that not everyone who professes to be a Christian is. Some are mistaken. Some are pretending. But, if all true believers persevere, why does Scripture so often encourage the saints to persevere and just as often warn them of the consequences of not persevering? If the saints persevere because they are Saints and cannot do otherwise, then no lack of exhortation or warning is going to prevent them from persevering.

And if one is not a Saint (i.e., elect), no amount of encouragement or warning is going to help them persevere in a faith they do not, cannot and should not have to persevere in. But nothing could be more obvious than this: Christians are repeatedly encouraged to persevere. Just as clearly they are warned of the consequences for not persevering throughout the pages of the New Testament. To challenge Perseverance of the Saints in the Calvinistic sense is not to deny *Eternal Security*, but to affirm Perseverance of the Saints in the Calvinistic sense, is to deny the believer *Assurance*.

Perseverance vs. Assurance

That is, if perseverance to the end is essential to prove you are truly one of the elect, you cannot know for sure that you are one of the elect until you make it to the end. It must also be stressed that a challenge to the Calvinistic view of Perseverance of the Saints is not to deny the importance of Saints persevering - even to the end. As already noted, Scripture is replete with exhortations and warnings regarding perseverance.

The problem with the Calvinistic view of perseverance is similar to the problem of the Arminian view of perseverance. That is, in Calvinism and Arminianism, justification and sanctification are hardly (if at all) distinguishable. In fact, some Calvinists refer to justification and sanctification as double justification. The Calvinist says if you do not persevere unto the end, you were never saved. The Arminian says that if you do not persevere to the end, you will lose your salvation. But neither can simply accept the record of Scripture that if you believe in the Lord Jesus Christ, you will be saved. Both, in effect, say that you must believe and must keep on believing in a way that manifests itself through perseverance to the end to be certain of your ultimate salvation.

Again, Calvinism denies the believer *assurance* whereas Arminianism denies the believer *security*. Thus, the problem with Calvinistic perseverance is not in its overemphasis, but in its mis-emphasis. Not only so, but a case can be made (perhaps somewhat ironically in light of the 5th point) for the fact that Calvinism actually and understandably results in an under-emphasis of sanctification. That is, since perseverance is supposedly a foregone conclusion for the elect, the one who believes he is elect is likely to pay less attention to exhortations and warnings about perseverance simply because if he is saved he *will* and if he is not saved he *can't*.

Since you cannot do anything about being elected or not elected, you cannot do anything about all that is inevitable because you are elected or not elected. This includes perseverance.

We *Ought* to Persevere

Perhaps by defining perseverance—at least as it is worked out behaviorally—as faithfully following Christ, or being obedient to God's Word, or walking in the *light*; we can see that perseverance is what *ought* to be true for every Christian. This is what believers are encouraged to do—and warned about failing to do—precisely because we have a tendency or inclination to not do it.

Consider the exhortation of Colossians 2:6 in which Paul says to the believers of the Colossian church:

As you therefore have received Christ Jesus as Lord so walk in Him.

Now if it is a foregone conclusion that a true believer will always continue to walk in Christ in the sense that Paul is speaking, why encourage him to do so? And what of Romans 12:1,2:

I urge you, therefore, brothers, by the mercies of God, to present your bodies as a living and holy sacrifice, acceptable to God...do not be conformed to this world, but be transformed, that you may prove what the will of God is, that which is good and acceptable and perfect.

It seems abundantly clear that Paul exhorts the believer this way because:

1. This is what the believer ought to do.

2. The believer without such exhortation is less inclined to do this.

Exhortations to Abide- Meaningless?

In John 15, where Jesus is talking to the disciples concerning their relationship to Him as the true vine, He exhorts them to abide in Him that they might bear fruit. He then, in verse 6, brings up the possibility of not abiding in Him and the subsequent consequences. This warning is totally meaningless and unnecessary if the Calvinistic position on Perseverance in correct.

Sproul, who spends a considerable amount of time defending the Calvinist view of perseverance, nevertheless reasons that:

If no one (i.e., among the elect) falls away, (or is even capable of falling away) why even bother to warn people against it?[103]

With this same thought in mind Sproul admits that:

It seems frivolous to warn people to avoid the impossible.[104]

---

[103] Ibid., 186.

[104] Ibid., 186.

While Sproul attempts to explain why it is not frivolous to warn people of the impossible, (i.e., encourage people that cannot do otherwise to persevere) he at least seems to understand why non-Calvinist's might find the Calvinistic view of perseverance fraught with problems.

In the opening verses of the second Epistle of Peter we read:

> *Simon Peter, a servant and apostle of Jesus Christ, to those who have obtained like precious faith with us by the righteousness of our God and Savior Jesus Christ: grace and peace be multiplied to you in the knowledge of God and of Jesus our Lord, as His divine power has given us all things that pertain to life and godliness, through the knowledge of Him who called us by glory and virtue, by which have given to us exceedingly great and precious promises, through these you might be partakers of the divine nature, having escaped the corruption that is in the world through lust. (2 Peter 1-4)*

Can there be any doubt that Peter is talking to true believers? And if true believers, can there be any doubt that they are truly saved?

Nevertheless, Peter goes on to exhort these same believers as follows:

> *But also for this very reason (the fact that they have escaped the corruption), giving all diligence, add to your faith virtue, to virtue knowledge, to knowledge self control, to self-control perseverance, to perseverance godliness, to godliness brotherly kindness, to brotherly kindness love. (5-7)*

Spiritual Building Materials

Obviously, the things they are told to add, including perseverance, are not necessarily added to the life of the true believer. If they were, there would be no need to exhort the believer to add them. To say they are not inevitable is not to say they are not important. Just the opposite. That is, that which will come to pass inevitably is nothing to be concerned about. If we can liken each of these additions to our faith as important building materials for a truly spiritual and productive life we can see why Peter says "giving all diligence add to your faith..." And of course this is exactly the point Peter is making and why he goes on to say:

> *For if these things are yours and abound, you will never be barren nor unfruitful in the knowledge of our Lord Jesus Christ. For he who lacks these things is shortsighted, even to blindness, and has forgotten that he was purged from his old sins. Therefore, brethren, be even more diligent to make your election and calling sure, for if you do these things you will never stumble; for so an entrance will be supplied to you abundantly into the everlasting kingdom of our Lord Jesus Christ. Therefore I will not be negligent to remind you always of these things, though you know them, and are established in the present truth. Yes, I think it is right, as long as I am in this tent to stir you up... (8-13).*

The Challenge and Goal

By reducing perseverance to an *inevitability* (as does the 5th point) all of these words of encouragement and warning are in a very real sense wasted. But in Scripture, *perseverance in holiness* to the end is seen as the challenge and goal of the

Christian life. It should not be taken for granted. To say that perseverance is what *we will* do because we are true believers is to radically redefine the meaning of perseverance. Instead we need to see perseverance as what we *ought to do* because we are true believers. God is more than able and always willing to help us persevere in holiness and faith. The question is, are we willing to let Him help us persevere?

Conclusion

*If the Calvinist is right and all the points stand and fall together,

*And if these points (properly understood) represent the entire system of Calvinism (soteriologically),

*Then it must also be true that if only one of these points can be proven scripturally unsound, the entire (soteriological) system must collapse.

In light of what we have just read from Scripture, I believe we have more than sufficient reason for rejecting Calvinism in general, and the Five Points of Calvinism in particular. Remember, a superstructure can be no more sure than the foundation upon which it rests.

Most leading Calvinists, such as those quoted in this book, go to great lengths to defend Calvinism from any and all attacks. They contend that Calvinism offers the only reasonable interpretation of Scripture with regard to matters relating to salvation. Some will even argue that Calvinism is not only intellectually satisfying for the thinking person, but that it answers the most questions and leaves the least questions unanswered. Some go so far as to say that all other views (such as the Arminian view) are not only heretical from a scriptural point of view, but that they are absurd from a philosophical and rational point of view. They say that only Calvinism can tell the beautiful and wonderful story of God's love, goodness, and grace.

Nevertheless, sometimes a Calvinist will admit (as we have already seen) the not so pleasant side of the Calvinist equation. Some will readily admit, as did Calvin, some of the more disturbing "truths" implied by a Calvinist view of such doctrines as reprobation. When Calvinists are not simply trying to put the best possible spin on Calvinism (which it seems they are so often trying to do) many will honestly face the difficulties of Calvinism. It is difficult for me to believe that in "unguarded moments" even the most staunch Calvinists do not engage in some soul searching about the implications of the Calvinist view. Speaking to this very issue, in a chapter titled, *God, Freedom, and Evil in Calvinist Thinking*, the Calvinist theologian, John S. Feinberg admits that,

> *Sometimes it would be easier not to be a Calvinist. An intellectual price tag comes with any conceptual scheme, but the one that comes with Calvinism seems beyond the resources of human intelligence to pay. Calvinists hold views that appear at very least counterintuitive. This is especially so with respect to Calvinist accounts of God's sovereign control in relation to human freedom and moral responsibility for evil.*

If Calvinists are right about divine sovereignty, there seems to be little room for human freedom. If freedom goes, so does human moral responsibility for sin. Worst of all, if Calvinists are right, it appears that God decides that there will be sin and evil in our world, maybe even brings it about that there is such evil, and yet, according to Calvinists, is not morally responsible for any of it. We are.

If this is Calvinism's God, Calvinism seems not only intellectually bankrupt but also religiously bankrupt. Who could worship this God? Moreover, if atheists understand this portrait of God as paradigmatic of traditional Christianity, no wonder they are repulsed by Christianity. Although committed atheists will not likely abandon their atheism for any concept of God, at least the Arminian portrayal of God seems more attractive than the Calvinist portrayal.[105]

While Fienberg, like Sproul, makes a valiant attempt at rescuing Calvinism for what it appears to be, there is nothing he says or could say to succeed at this monumental task. The truth is that Calvinism is what it appears to be. Therefore, rejecting Calvinism makes much more sense than trying to rescue it.

---

[105] Edited by Thomas R. Schreiner and Bruce A. Ware, *The Grace of God, the Bondage of the Will*, Vol. 2 (Grand Rapids, MI: Baker Books), Chapter 20, by John S. Fienberg, page 459.

The Lazy Man's Guide to Understanding Calvinism

The Five Points Say	The Scriptures Say
You must be... Born again so you can believe. Thus, faith is a *consequence* or *result* of regeneration.	You must... Believe so that you can be born again. Thus, faith is the *precondition* of or *requirement* for regeneration. John 1:12,13
You are... Elected by God *without* regard to faith in Christ.	You are... Elected by God in accordance *with* faith in Christ. John 3:16, 17
Christ died *only* for the *elect*.	Christ died for *all* the *lost*. 1 John 2:2
God *appears* to offer salvation to all—i.e., the general and outward call—but only intends to save some (the elect), and insures that the some He intends to save will be saved—i.e., the efficacious or inner call—without regard to the faith or willingness of the elect. The elect cannot help but believe and be eventually saved, and the unelect cannot help but not believe and be ultimately damned.	God *truly* offers salvation to everyone on the condition they receive and believe in Jesus Christ. The saved can thank God for the provision of salvation (the cross), the offer of salvation (the gospel proclamation), the nature of the offer (a free gift), and the capacity to believe in Christ and thereby receive the free gift. Those ultimately lost will have only themselves to blame. Rom. 1:16
The saved *will* persevere in holiness and faith to the end of their life on earth, thereby proving they are among the elect. Those who do not persevere in faith and holiness until the end have proved they were never saved and therefore not among the elect.	The saved *should* persevere in faith and holiness to the end of their life on earth, thereby proving their love for the Lord. The truly saved, to the degree they fail to persevere in faith and holiness, have to that same degree demonstrated a lack of love for the Lord. Although saved, they experience a loss of fellowship with the Lord in this life, and a loss of rewards in the next. John 15:1-14

An Even Lazier Man's Guide to Understanding Calvinism

YOU WILL BE SAVED OR DAMNED *FOR* ALL ETERNITY BECAUSE YOU WERE SAVED OR DAMNED *FROM* ALL ETERNITY.